AN INSTITUTE OF DIRECTORS
PUBLICATION

THE DIRECTOR'S HANDBOOK

your duties,
responsibilities
and liabilities

edited by

Martin Webster

IN ASSOCIATION WITH

Pinsent Masons

Published by Director Publications Ltd for the Institute of Directors, 116 Pall Mall, London SW1Y 5ED.

Published in association with Pinsent Masons, CityPoint, One Ropemaker Street, London EC2Y 9AH.

Distributed by Kogan Page Ltd, 120 Pentonville Road, London N1 9JN.

First published in 2005;
Second edition 2007.

A CIP record for this book is available from the British Library.

ISBN: 978-0-7494-4982-7

Designed by Halo Design, London. Printed and bound in Great Britain by The Westdale Press Ltd.

contents

introduction

A brief guide to the basic principles underlying the law's treatment of companies and to some of the key rules under the Companies Act 2006.

Describes the various types of company and includes information on:

- ☐ the legal constitution of a company – the memorandum and articles of association
- ☐ the rights of shareholders
- ☐ the role of the company secretary
- ☐ the role and appointment of auditors
- ☐ board meetings and resolutions
- ☐ shares and share issues

duties

Looks at the core legal obligations of directors to the company and to shareholders and others.

Covers:

- ☐ fiduciary duties
- ☐ the legal positions of executives, non-executives and shadow directors
- ☐ the code of directors' duties in the Companies Act 2006
- ☐ remedies when duties are breached
- ☐ liability for directors' reports
- ☐ health and safety duties
- ☐ corporate manslaughter
- ☐ competition law

acknowledgements

In compiling the second edition of this book, I have had the help of several expert authors. Chapters that have been written by or contain contributions from my colleagues at Pinsent Masons include:

- [ ] service contracts   **Robert Mecrate-Butcher**
- [ ] pensions   **Nicola Bumpus and Alastair Meeks**
- [ ] remuneration issues   **Rory Cray**
- [ ] insolvency and financial difficulty   **Jonathan Jeffries and Dawn Allen**

I am grateful for other valuable material from **Jeremy Phillips**, **Simon Gronow** and **Alan Davis**, and indeed for the help and support of all my partners and colleagues at the firm.

The task would not have been completed without the encouragement and enthusiasm of Tom Nash and his team at Director Publications. Of particular note are the stylish cover and layout created by Gary Parfitt of Halo Design and the formidable sub-editing of Caroline Proud, who curbed my wilder excesses with a skill and tact that are largely responsible for the lucid and reasoned text I hope you now find before you.

Martin Webster
Pinsent Masons
London, April 2007

EXECUTIVE DIRECTOR

A FTSE 100 company wishes to appoint a marketing director to the board. Applicants must be committed to the highest possible professional standards and should either hold the IoD Diploma in Company Direction or be willing to undertake the programme on appointment. The successful candidate will be expected to go on to qualify as a chartered director.

FINANCE DIRECTOR

A medium-sized organisation is looking for a finance director to join its board. The successful candidate will be a qualified accountant with a proven track record of delivering profitable growth. He or she will not only help manage risks but also spot opportunities – making a significant contribution to the strategic development of the business. A chartered director is preferred.

CHAIRMAN

An international company requires a new chairman to lead the board and ensure effective communication with institutional investors and other shareholders. Only candidates who are chartered directors or hold the IoD Diploma in Company Direction will be considered.

NON-EXECUTIVE DIRECTOR

A major PLC is looking for a new non-executive director. The successful candidate will be an experienced NED, respected by the City and institutional investors. He or she will add value to the decision-making process, playing a vital role in the development of boardroom strategy and policy. Only chartered directors need apply.

CHIEF EXECUTIVE

A not-for-profit organisation is looking for an experienced CEO to guide it through a period of restructuring and regional expansion. The role demands leadership skills of the highest possible quality; proven commitment to the principles of good corporate governance is essential. The ideal candidate is a chartered director.

COMPANY SECRETARY

A FTSE 250 company is looking for a company secretary with the experience and confidence to work with a main board consisting entirely of chartered directors. The successful candidate will play an important part in the development of boardroom strategy and ensure compliance with all legal and regulatory requirements. Preference will be given to a chartered secretary who has also qualified as a chartered director.

The job ads of the future will read something like this.

Chartered Director is the IoD's professional qualification for directors and has the endorsement and support of government, regulators, the investment community, executive search agencies and many companies in the FTSE 100.

Without it, you'll look like an amateur.

a new framework for the new economy

Company directors collectively help to promote confidence in corporate Britain; their decisions ultimately have an impact on the UK economy. In order to make the UK the best place in the world to start and build a company, government must work in partnership with business, creating the conditions for success and helping the UK respond to the challenge of globalisation.

The DTI's role is to improve the competitiveness of the UK in the global market. We are committed to ensuring that the legal and regulatory framework within which business operates promotes enterprise and growth and provides the right conditions for investment and employment. A robust yet flexible company law framework is one of the essential ingredients of a successful and competitive economy.

The Companies Act 2006 is part of a wider programme of reform to facilitate enterprise, encourage investment and promote long-term company performance in the UK. This handbook helps directors to understand better their role and responsibilities under it.

The Act brings together in one place company law legislation from 1985 to the 2004 Companies Audit, Investigations and Community Enterprise Act, and introduces significant changes to simplify and improve the law. It is easier to understand and more flexible than its predecessors, with a separate "code" of accounting and reporting requirements for small companies.

All companies can now make greater use of more efficient electronic communications with shareholders, and the enhanced business review requirements will promote higher quality narrative reporting by quoted companies. The Act also includes a statutory statement of directors' duties, which provides greater clarity about what is expected of business leaders.

I very much welcome this revised edition of *The Director's Handbook* and the IoD's continuing efforts to keep company directors up to date with developments in company law and governance and to raise the overall quality of directorship. I am sure that those who use the handbook will find it a valuable and reliable source of information and guidance.

The Rt Hon Alistair Darling MP
Secretary of State for Trade and Industry

manual for the modern director

The vast majority of directors know that for their businesses to succeed they need to combine entrepreneurialism and risk-taking with professionalism and integrity. That means complying with the law and following best practice.

UK businesses can only achieve their full competitive potential if those running them are up to the task. Businesses may find that their cost of capital is affected by being able to demonstrate clear understanding of the framework of company law. Today, an ever-greater emphasis is being placed on relationships with shareholders and other stakeholders. Investors want to be sure their interests are protected; employees want to work for businesses that are aware of their responsibilities to communities and the environment; customers expect increasingly high standards – their loyalty is hard to win and easy to lose.

The difficulty for many people in business is finding accessible sources of information and support.

The IoD exists to support, represent and set standards for UK directors. Underlying these three goals is that of making UK businesses more successful and more competitive. We represent the interests of directors to government and others, and are trying to achieve regulatory regimes that complement (rather than impede) well-run businesses. We are the premier provider of training and development for directors: our Chartered Director qualification, the world's first accredited qualification for directors, is endorsed by increasing numbers of major institutions.

We want to raise the standards of directorship but, at the same time, we know how complex the task can be. We know that the burden of regulation is one of the main concerns of our members, most of whom run SMEs without the benefit of specialist in-house teams to guide them through the potential minefields. Directors frequently feel very much alone. Even when government sets out to simplify the rules, the sheer volume of regulation can seem overwhelming.

Directors cannot plead ignorance of the law as it affects them and their companies. But few of them can reasonably be expected to be legal experts; changes in the law can easily catch them out.

To help fill the information gap and provide practical support for those running businesses, we publish *The Director's Handbook*. Since the first edition came out in 2005, there has been a major reform of UK company law in the shape of the Companies Act 2006 – at exactly 1,300 sections, reputedly the largest single piece of legislation ever. The Act, coming into force in stages up to October 2008 will affect all companies, large and small. While much of the law has not changed in substance, there are important new provisions such as the statutory statement of directors' duties, rules on derivative actions and significant changes in the regime for private companies.

Directors need to be able to realise when it is appropriate to seek professional help – and to be able to understand the advice they are given. This second edition of the handbook guides them through some of the complexities of the 2006 Act. Like its predecessor, it is an invaluable source of information and advice across a wide range of issues. We are again delighted with the efforts of Martin Webster and the team at Pinsent Masons, who have succeeded in producing a guide to law and good practice that is both authoritative and accessible.

This is not intended to be a legal textbook, but a work for directors to use in their business lives. It draws on real examples, with which many directors will be familiar, to make its points.

Although this book is primarily aimed at directors of companies incorporated under the Companies Acts, much of the subject matter is also of relevance to many other types of organisation – be they in the private, public or voluntary sectors. I believe that even those parts that at first glance seem to relate only to listed companies are of wider general interest. Chapter 3, for example, on the Combined Code on Corporate Governance, addresses issues that are fundamentally important to all organisations and of interest to anyone who has pension or other investments.

I hope that you will find this book as useful and informative as I have; I commend it to you.

Miles Templeman
Director General, Institute of Directors

preface

This book is designed to be a practical guide for all those who are directors of companies or perform an equivalent role. It is neither a legal text book nor an exhaustive statement of the law as it applies to directors; rather, it aims to be an accessible source of advice and best practice for people who face real issues in their daily working lives.

In planning this book, we wanted to cover a number of specific areas where directors commonly encounter risk in fulfilling their responsibilities. All of the authors are practising lawyers who each day advise directors of their rights and liabilities and help them in finding practical answers to problems. We hope the chapters that follow are a distillation of that advice and help and will be a real resource for those who run companies and need to understand the ever-changing legal and regulatory environment in which they operate.

This second edition takes account of the Companies Act 2006. Although, as I write, most of that mammoth piece of legislation is not yet in force, we have in large part anticipated its introduction, so that we describe the law as it is or will be rather than as it was. The implementation timetable in the appendix provides more detail.

Except as specifically mentioned, the law is stated as at April 1, 2007.

Martin Webster
Pinsent Masons
London, April 2007

introduction

CHAPTER 1

1. Basic principles of company law

Companies come in many different shapes and sizes; there are key differences in what they can and cannot do, and the purpose for which each is designed. But all are **separate legal persons** independent of their directors and shareholders. Only rarely will the law look behind a company and treat it as being the same person as those who control it.

This concept of a company as a separate legal personality has two consequences:

☐ a company's property belongs to it and not to its directors, management or shareholders. Even if you are a sole director and a 100 per cent shareholder, you can still be found guilty of stealing from your own company. Liquidators and future owners will have an interest in pursuing claims for theft or misuse of assets where a company has been plundered by those in day to day control. Robert Maxwell was only the most prominent of company chairmen to forget this basic principle.

☐ a company is responsible for its own debts and liabilities. The shareholders and, as a general rule, directors cannot be forced to pay them.

That second point is why "limited" companies give their shareholders **"limited liability"**. A **limited company** may be sued until all its assets have been exhausted, but no creditor can turn to the shareholders and ask them to meet any deficit. Once a company has received at least the nominal value of its issued shares (£1 for a £1 share etc), the shares are "fully paid" and the shareholder has no further liability. Shares may be issued "partly paid": a £1 share may be issued with 25p payable on issue and 75p at some future date or on an earlier liquidation. But once those amounts are paid in full, the shareholder has no further liability for the company's debts.

These basic principles underlie much of what follows in this book. But it is important to remember they are principles of company law. In the field of tax in particular, many inroads have been made by both statute and the courts that allow the authorities to look behind company structures at who really owns and controls the entity.

Most companies are "limited by shares", and they may be "private" or "public" companies. Public companies may have their shares "listed" or traded on a stock exchange – although they are under no obligation to do so.

If a company is not limited by shares, it may be "limited by guarantee", or it may be unlimited. All of these different types of company are explained below.

2. Different types of company

Private limited company

All companies that are not public companies are defined by law as private. Being a private company is the default position. Private companies can range from substantial trading entities that are subsidiaries of public companies in large groups to small family companies – or just a trading vehicle for one or two individuals who want the benefit of limited liability. As such, the private company is a very flexible format that can be adapted to fit numerous different requirements. But the one thing that a private company cannot do as a matter of law is offer its shares to the public. Any private company that wants to issue shares to the public must first become a plc or public limited company.

Private companies will, therefore, usually have fewer shareholders than a public company, and there will often be restrictions on the transfer of their shares. Those with a very small number of shareholders, including those that are subsidiaries, might ban all transfers of shares that are not first approved by the board of directors. This allows the board to control who becomes a shareholder and, ultimately, who controls the company.

Companies with a larger shareholder base might have more sophisticated rules that allow the transfer of shares by a shareholder but first require that they are offered to existing shareholders (under "pre-emption provisions"), thereby giving them the opportunity to keep ownership within the existing group and to exclude new shareholders.

Some private companies are, of course, effectively vehicles for sole traders who may be keen to have the protection of limited liability, or who may simply enjoy an added kudos from trading as a company.

Public limited company

If you want to be a public rather than a private company, you must take a number of steps. You will need:

☐   a name that ends with the words "public limited company" (or the Welsh equivalent); permitted abbreviations are PLC, plc or Plc.

☐   an allotted share capital with a nominal value of at least £50,000 and paid up share capital of at least £12,500 (or, from April 2008, the equivalent in euros). You could, for example, allot 50,000 £1 shares, or 250,000 20p shares, each issued and paid at least to one quarter of its nominal value – 50,000 £1 shares paid up as to 25p on each share, or 250,000 20p shares paid up as to 5p on each share. (There is no equivalent minimum for a private company.)

A public company is subject to more stringent controls than a private one in a number of areas. Some of them are listed below.

☐　The rules on making loans to directors are more restrictive for all companies in a group where one of the members is a public company (see section 9 in chapter 7).

☐　A public company can purchase or redeem its own shares, but it can only pay for them by using those profits from which dividends can be paid. A private company, on the other hand, has the option of using its capital if distributable profits fall short.

☐　There has for many years been a general prohibition on companies providing financial assistance for the purchase of their own shares. A breach is a criminal offence. That has created problems for private equity transactions and group banking arrangements in particular. From October 2008, the Companies Act 2006 lifts this ban for private companies – but not for public ones.

☐　Many private companies are allowed to prepare abbreviated accounts each year. Public companies, on the other hand, have to prepare and file with Companies House a full set of accounts, and pay the added costs that may involve.

☐　All public companies are subject to the Takeover Code, whether their shares are publicly traded or not. The Code regulates the ways offers to acquire a public company are made, and the Companies Act 2006 has now put it on a statutory footing.

Listed companies

A public company may have its shares admitted to the Official List of the UK Listing Authority (that is, the Financial Services Authority), with its shares traded on the London Stock Exchange: it will then be said to be a "listed" or "quoted" company. One may also talk about a company's shares being traded on other markets in London – including the Alternative Investment Market (AIM) and PLUS (the former OFEX) – or anywhere else in the world.

Having your shares traded on a public market will inevitably bring increased obligations for directors – be they statutory or regulatory. Many of these obligations are explained in the later chapters of this book.

THE COMPANIES ACT 2006: THE LAW REFORMED

After a nine-year process of reports, committees and consultations, the Companies Act 2006 finally saw the light of day and received Royal Assent in November 2006. Despite all that preparation, the final afternoon of debate in the House of Lords still had 1,029 amendments to vote on (of which only 13 were debated).

One reason for that last-minute rush was the decision to consolidate the remaining parts of the 1985 Companies Act into the new statute, so that we have one code of UK company law in one "place".

Though sensible, such consolidation creates a door-stopper of an Act – in fact, the longest Act ever passed by the Westminster Parliament, or any parliament anywhere in the world.

What was the inspiration behind the reform? The government highlighted four key objectives:

☐ enhancing shareholder engagement and a long-term investment culture;

☐ ensuring better regulation and a "think small first" approach;

☐ making it easier to set up and run a company;

☐ providing flexibility for the future.

Responses to the Act have, perhaps inevitably, been mixed. At 1,300 sections and 16 schedules, it's hardly the best advertisement for a "less is more", "think small first" approach. And, while much of the bureaucracy surrounding small businesses has been stripped away, "better regulation" tends to see it creep back in for the larger company.

Few would deny, however, that the Act is better drafted and better organised than its predecessors. And, in the context of the board, it merely enshrines in law those things that a director should have been doing anyway – namely, thinking about the long-term interests of shareholders and other stakeholders in the 21st century.

Directors' obligations under the Act are discussed in detail in the next chapter. The key changes in the Act, and the dates of their implementation, are listed in the appendix, see page 199.

Holding companies and subsidiaries

If company A owns more than 50 per cent of the issued shares of company B, it is clear that A is B's holding company and B is therefore a subsidiary of A. But the definition of "subsidiary" and "holding company" in the Companies Act goes beyond that simple example and covers a number of other situations. B will be a subsidiary of A if:

☐   A holds a majority of voting rights in B – it is voting rights, not just shares, that are important;

☐   A is a shareholder of B and has the right to appoint and remove a majority of the directors;

☐   A is a shareholder of B and controls a majority of the voting rights in B as a result of an agreement it has with other shareholders.

Other key points include:

☐   A company that is a subsidiary of B also counts as a subsidiary of A.

☐   B will be a "wholly owned subsidiary" of A if it has no shareholders other than A and A's other subsidiaries or nominees acting on A's behalf.

☐   Shares held in B on behalf of A are treated as being held by A.

☐   Shares held in a trust for others do not count: if B holds shares in A as trustee of, say, A's pension fund, it will not be treated as owning shares in A. (Generally, a subsidiary cannot hold shares in its own holding company.)

A company with more than one trading activity has the choice of carrying on all its trades under the umbrella of one company or splitting them between a number of trading subsidiaries. Its decision will probably depend on the factors below.

☐   **Risk mitigation** – having a number of companies in the group with the benefits of limited liability can be an advantage. If one subsidiary gets into financial difficulties there is nothing in law that obliges its parent to continue supporting it, unless it has guaranteed the subsidiary's liabilities or otherwise agreed to help.

☐   **Tax** – as a general rule, whatever trading structure is used, the effect should be tax neutral, but there are numerous examples where some advantage, or disadvantage, can arise from putting separate activities into separate subsidiaries and carrying out transactions between them. Some tax reliefs may depend on whether there is a 51 per cent or 75 per cent relationship with the group companies involved.

☐   **Administration** – the more companies you have, the greater the administrative burden, the greater the cost and the more paper is generated.

In addition to its definitions of subsidiary and holding company, the Companies Act introduces definitions, for accounting purposes, of **"subsidiary undertaking"** and **"parent undertaking"**. These are wider definitions and encompass not only ordinary subsidiaries and holding companies but also other situations where there is effective control and the accounts of two or more companies should be consolidated. They can also include entities other than companies – such as partnerships and unincorporated associations.

Guarantee and unlimited companies and limited liability partnerships

Companies limited by guarantee are often found in the not-for-profit, charity or non-trading sectors, though there is no restriction on the use to which they can be put. Such companies have guarantors rather than shareholders. These guarantors are members who agree to make a limited contribution towards the payment of the company's debts in the event of winding up. That limit is usually fixed at a nominal £1 and is only required if the company's assets fall short.

A guarantee company may drop the word "limited" from its name if, but only if, it exists for charitable purposes or to promote other good causes and there is a ban on the payment of any dividends to its members (and, on a winding up, any surplus goes to a body with a similar purpose).

Different again are **unlimited companies**. Here, the liability of members is truly unlimited and they can be required to pay the company's debts without limit if it defaults and is wound up. Of course, for the shareholders of many small companies the concept of limited liability is at times notional – banks and landlords will often require personal guarantees of a company's liabilities. So an unlimited company may be no more than an acceptance of a reality, and it will carry the big advantage of secrecy: there is generally no obligation to file accounts at Companies House.

Since 2000, there has been an entirely new legal entity – a limited liability partnership. An LLP is often the vehicle used by large firms of lawyers and accountants to enjoy both the tax benefits of a partnership and the limited liability of a company. In most respects, it is more akin to a company than anything else, but legally it is a new concept and is governed solely by statute. The main quid pro quo for limited liability is the obligation to file annual accounts at Companies House.

3. Company constitution

Every company will have two documents that comprise its constitution: a **memorandum of association** and **articles of association**. Both will usually keep to a fairly standard format, but the detail of what they say can assume great importance. Big changes are due in this area in October 2008 as a result of the Companies Act 2006.

Memorandum

A company's memorandum might be the least regarded of its key documents, rarely looked at save by pedantic lawyers. Nonetheless, historically it has played a crucial role: a company has only been able to do those things its memorandum says it can (unlike a "natural person", who has complete freedom to do what they like unless the law says otherwise).

As a result, the memorandum, and more specifically its objects clause, will usually be drawn in very broad terms. It is likely to start with a description of what it is intended the company will actually do: run an airline in the case of British Airways; operate a bank if HSBC. After that, there will usually be a list of 20 or 30 subsidiary objects or powers going well beyond what the company might ever contemplate doing.

The memorandum will also set out the company's name in full, and state whether the registered office of the company is to be in England and Wales, Wales alone or Scotland. Lastly, it will give the initial amount of the company's share capital.

The point of the objects clause has been to exclude the possibility of a company acting *ultra vires*, that is beyond its proper powers, potentially putting the directors who authorised the offending action at risk of breaching their duties.

(*Ultra vires* actions once carried risks for lenders, too – leaving them with no enforceable security and no way of recovering their money if the company became insolvent. That problem was largely solved by legislative changes providing that if a third party, for example, a bank lending money, acted in good faith, it was not to be prejudiced by any deficiency in a company's constitution.)

Shareholders have been able to take action to stop directors acting outside the company's objects and directors have, potentially at least, been personally liable when they do.

Under the Companies Act 2006, however, the position is very different. After one failed attempt at reform in 1989, the Act cuts through the legal undergrowth and simply (with effect from October 2008) removes the objects wholesale from the memorandum, along with most of the rest of the document. The memorandum is reduced to a bald statement that the initial subscribers wish to form a company and agree to become members and take at least one share each. It is no more than it says: a "memorandum" of that initial agreement and, beyond that, it has no useful purpose.

Only if the articles contain some specific restriction will the company be limited in its actions. That will be the case with a company that is a charity, where the objects will at least be restricted to a charitable purpose, and it may also apply to a joint venture company where the parties to the joint venture may want to specify the purpose for which they have come together and funded the company. In general, though, a company will be able to be formed and used for any legal purpose without anyone worrying whether it has the right objects or powers in its constitution.

One note of caution: directors need to use these unfettered powers to promote the success of the company, not for some extraneous purpose (see chapter 2, section 7). So transactions that have no commercial benefit, such as gifts or a guarantee of another's liabilities, might still be vulnerable.

It is not only new companies that are affected by the change. Come October 2008, all existing companies will have their constitutions automatically amended. Everything apart from the basic agreement to form the company and take shares will be lifted from the memorandum and dumped into the articles. Once there, it can be amended or deleted as the shareholders wish, and many will no doubt want to get rid of the lengthy objects clauses as a first step.

Articles

The articles of association, the second part of a company's constitution, comprise its internal regulations or by-laws. They set out both the way the company is to be run and the rights between shareholders. It is the articles that deal with subjects such as the rights attached to each class of share, the quorum for a meeting and the way to transfer shares. With effect from October 2008, they also contain any restrictions on what the company can do (whether imported from the memorandum or inserted afresh).

Companies legislation sets out a model form of articles known as Table A. (There are alternative models for a company limited by guarantee and other types of company.) Many private companies will use Table A as the basis for their articles and make a few amendments to suit their particular circumstances. A company's articles may thus comprise a page or two of these amendments and otherwise incorporate the statutory Table A by reference (often not setting it out in full, leaving shareholders to find a copy elsewhere).

The Companies Act 2006 brings in new model forms of articles for a variety of different types of company. Designed for the 21st century, they are shorter than the old versions and drafted in plain English.

Larger or public companies are more likely to exclude Table A and instead set out the entirety of their articles in one document. In practice, even they will follow Table A in many instances, but the changes will be more sophisticated when compared with those used by a private company.

You can put in your articles whatever you want, subject to one proviso: you cannot go against the law. For example, the Companies Act says a company can only pay a dividend if it has distributable profits, and the articles cannot improve on that. Similarly, statute says that shareholders can always remove a director by passing an ordinary resolution – the articles can make it easier to get rid of a board member, but they cannot contradict the statute by making it more difficult.

Stock Exchange or AIM traded companies must comply with certain rules as a condition of being listed. And if the articles of a fully listed company have any "unusual features" they must first be approved by the UK Listing Authority (that is, the Financial Services Authority).

It is often said that the articles are a contract between a company and its members. When you become a shareholder you do so subject to the terms of the company's articles – now and in the future. You will have the opportunity to vote on any change but, once "passed", a change, whether you approve of it or not, is, in principle, binding. The corollary is that a shareholder can go to court to stop a company acting in a way that is contrary to its articles.

Just as you can put into your articles what you want, you can change them at any time. To do so, requires a special resolution (see page 21). Changes, however, will be open to challenge if they cannot be justified as being in good faith or are partisan. If a majority of shareholders are motivated by malice and push through a change harmful to the minority, a court might overturn the change as not being in the interests of the company as a whole.

A company's articles are a public document. They must be filed at Companies House. So they are not the place to put details that a private company might want to keep confidential – a financial return to be enjoyed by a shareholder, for example, or detailed voting arrangements. Shareholders in joint venture companies or in private equity investments might opt to keep these details private. That might mean that a company's articles do not tell the whole story of the relationship between shareholders and their company – other documents might be needed for the full picture.

Board of directors and board committees

We look in more detail at directors in section 4 below, and at their duties and responsibilities in the next chapter. And in chapter 3 we look at corporate governance, in which directors have a major role to play. But for now it is worth highlighting one provision found in most articles (using here the wording from the proposed new Table A, effective from October 2008): **"the directors are responsible for the management of the company's business, for which purpose they may exercise all the powers of the company"**.

That encapsulates the directors' authority, the basis for the power they exercise. It protects them, and the company, from interference by shareholders in the day to day management of the company. If the shareholders do not like what the directors are doing, they can remove them or, less drastically, pass a special resolution giving them a particular direction. Or they can change the articles to limit the directors' powers. Neither course of action is commonly seen in practice, though an implied threat by shareholders to remove directors can have the desired effect.

Just as shareholders effectively delegate the management of a company to its directors, those directors, acting together as a board, will be permitted by the articles to delegate day to day decision making to individual executive directors and to committees of the main board. Some committees may be a permanent feature, required by governance considerations – for example, remuneration or audit committees – others may be more ad hoc and formed to see through a particular deal or issue (see section 14 of chapter 3).

Delegation to individual executive directors may be by means of board resolution but executives' service contracts may also set out clearly what their duties are and what authority they have.

4. Company personnel

Shareholders

For all companies with a share capital, the terms "shareholders" and "members" are interchangeable. But whichever term is used, it will refer to the person who has the legal ownership of a share – that is the person who is shown in the company's register of members as holding the share. That person may just be a nominee and be quite different from the person who has beneficial ownership.

Legally, a company has had no need to pay regard to the beneficial owners of its shares and it may be quite unaware of who they are (although it may, in certain circumstances, be able to force disclosure of their identity); it has concerned itself only with those persons its register shows as being members.

Keen, however, to "enhance shareholder engagement", the government has changed the rules. Under the Companies Act 2006, beneficial owners of shares (including anyone who owns shares through a PEP, ISA or similar vehicle) are, with effect from October 2007, able to exercise many of the rights attaching to their shares.

For the rights of beneficial owners to be recognised:

☐   a company must amend its articles accordingly;

☐   the registered shareholder must "nominate" the beneficial owner who is to enjoy these rights.

If these provisos are not met, it remains the case that only shareholders named in the register can vote, receive dividends and exercise other shareholder rights. And only they can enforce rights against the company; the beneficial owner cannot bring a direct claim.

The shareholders are the owners of the company. They ultimately control what it does by virtue of their ability to remove and appoint directors and to change the articles. Their rights and obligations as shareholders will usually be set out in the articles, backed up by the Companies Act and the law as developed by judges in decided cases.

There may also be a shareholders' agreement that sets out terms agreed between the shareholders; or in a 50:50 company, a joint venture agreement that sets out how deadlocks between shareholders are to be settled. A company that has received private equity or venture capital funding may have an investment agreement that also deals with the rights between various groups of shareholders. But unlike the articles, these agreements will only bind those shareholders who sign up to them originally or who do so when they become shareholders and put their name to some form of deed of adherence. The articles, by contrast, apply to all who have acquired shares at any time, whether they have specifically agreed to them or not.

Directors

We have looked already at the role directors play as the individuals to whom the management of the company is delegated by shareholders. But who exactly are the directors? Is it just those given the name, or can it include others? The Companies Act 2006 (s.250) says that "director" includes "any person occupying the position of director, by whatever name called". So you might be called "governor" or "trustee" and actually be a director. (Conversely, a director of sales or general director might not be a member of the board at all.) So it is the role you perform, not the title you are given, that determines whether you are a director or not.

In some circumstances, references to a director may include a **"shadow director"**, someone defined as a "person in accordance with whose directions or instructions the directors of a company are accustomed to act" (Companies Act 2006, s.251(1)). Note that the shadow director's influence has to be over the whole board, or at least a majority of it, not just one or two directors; and there has to be some history of influence, not just an isolated occurrence. Professional advisers, such as lawyers and accountants, are specifically excluded, as are parent companies in certain circumstances. But dominant shareholders, company doctors sent in to implement a corporate recovery plan, and even banks seeking to protect their loans to a company, are potential shadow directors.

Not every reference in companies legislation to a director covers a shadow director as well: there must be specific wording to include a shadow director. Most importantly, a shadow director can be liable for wrongful trading when a company becomes insolvent (see section 4 of chapter 8).

In many smaller companies, directors will continue in office until they voluntarily resign or are forcibly removed. Larger companies and all listed companies will require directors to **"retire by rotation"** at the AGM (for example, a third of the directors might retire each year), and directors newly appointed by the board must retire at the following AGM. They then stand for re-election, when shareholders usually vote them back in. (In November 2004, one notable exception to this was seen in Malcolm Glazer's battle to take control of Manchester United – he held enough shares to defeat the resolution to re-appoint three of the retiring directors.)

The Combined Code on Corporate Governance, applicable to listed companies, requires that all directors, executive and non-executive, should stand for re-election at least once every three years (see section 13 of chapter 3).

Company secretary

All companies must have a secretary and, if there is only one director, he or she cannot also be the secretary. That remains the rule until April 2008, when private companies will be able to drop the role if they wish. But if there is a job to be done and you want to call the person who does it company secretary, you can carry on as before.

With the increasing focus in recent years on corporate governance, the role of the company secretary has grown in importance. In many ways, the secretary is now seen as the guardian of the company's proper compliance with both the law and best practice.

In a public company, the directors must take all reasonable steps to have a secretary with particular previous experience or a particular qualification or, as a catch all, one who appears "to the directors to be capable of discharging" the functions of a secretary because of previous experience or qualifications (Companies Act 2006, s.273). In practice, secretaries of most listed and AIM companies will have an appropriate formal qualification. Private company secretaries (where they continue) are not required to have any particular qualification or experience.

The secretary can be appointed and removed by the directors, though any related employment rights he or she might have should not be forgotten. The Combined Code for listed companies makes it clear that the dismissal of a company secretary should be a question for the whole board, not just the chairman or chief executive. That is consistent with today's view that the secretary is the servant of the entire board and, as such, might sometimes be in the position of giving advice that is unpalatable to the executive directors. In addition, all directors should have access to the advice of the company secretary.

The secretary is an officer of the company and his or her duties can be wide ranging. They are not all set out in companies legislation and will differ from company to company. Useful guidance notes on the duties of the secretary, however, can be found on the website of the Institute of Chartered Secretaries and Administrators (ICSA). As an officer of the company, the secretary can bind the company in the same way as a director. Like a director, he or she owes fiduciary duties to the company, must act in good faith and avoid any conflict of interest (see chapters 2 and 7 for equivalent duties for directors).

Auditors

It used to be a requirement for every company to have auditors who, each year, would examine and report on the company's accounts and confirm whether they complied with companies legislation and whether they gave a "true and fair view" of the company. More recently, many smaller companies have been relieved of this requirement, though they must still prepare and file accounts.

A detailed description of the duties of an auditor is beyond the scope of this chapter, but it is worth noting that, if the auditor fails in its duties, it may be liable for any loss the failure has caused, both to the company and to its shareholders. In some cases, it may also be liable to third parties who have relied on the audit report – though recent case law has provided some limit on auditors' exposure.

Not surprisingly, since the collapse of Arthur Andersen as part of the Enron scandal, and Equitable Life's multi-million pound claim against Ernst and Young (albeit unsuccessful), auditors have been looking at ways to limit their liability. Until the Companies Act 2006, any limitation in respect of an audit was void and unenforceable. From April 2008, that changes, and an auditor will be able to agree with a company each year a cap on its liability for the audit. Not only must the finance director agree, but the shareholders must approve the limitation at the AGM. Even then, when any claim against the auditors comes to court, the judge can substitute a higher amount if that would be "fair and reasonable".

Auditors will always rightly point out that they do not prepare the accounts on which they report: that is the job of the directors. In practice, though, they may help smaller companies put the accounts together – as a general rule, the smaller the business, the greater the level of assistance.

The accountancy firms provide numerous services to their clients above and beyond the basic audit. Governance principles suggest that the auditor might have a conflict of interest in doing commercial work in addition to its audit duties (see section 15 of chapter 3), and statute requires that details of non-audit services are disclosed in the annual report. At the same time, however, the involvement of auditors has been extended with the requirement for them to check some of the factual information in the directors' remuneration report (see chapter 6).

Who hires and fires auditors? The directors appoint the first auditors of a company and can fill any vacancy that arises between general meetings. Apart from that, the auditors are appointed by a resolution of shareholders at each annual general meeting, and there are special notice provisions (see page 20) where the auditor to be appointed is not the same firm appointed at the previous AGM.

An auditor can be removed by ordinary resolution of the shareholders but, again, there are special safeguards in the legislation that have to be observed.

A resigning auditor must produce a statement setting out any circumstances connected with the resignation that should be brought to shareholders' attention. Alternatively, if there are no such circumstances, that fact must be stated. This is designed to prevent auditors who are unhappy with any aspect of the accounts departing quietly and keeping the problems to themselves. Concerns must be stated frankly. Additional safeguards aim to protect the company from the risk of defamatory material being circulated.

5. Company meetings

Board meetings

As we have seen above, the articles of a company will delegate the management of the company to its board of directors. The board will act collectively, meeting regularly to consider and decide issues affecting the company. How those board meetings are run is a matter largely for the articles and for the board itself to decide. Unlike shareholders' meetings, which are more tightly regulated, board meetings are generally free of legislative interference.

So there is nothing in statute about the notice to be given for board meetings. Any director or the secretary can call a board meeting and, unless the articles or a previous board meeting have stipulated the length of notice to be given, the only requirement is that it be reasonable.

What is reasonable will depend on the type of company and its past practice. For a private company where all directors are already on site, reasonable notice may be a few hours or even minutes; for a large international company with directors scattered over the globe and non-executives with other responsibilities, board meetings will be fixed a year or more in advance. Again, unless the articles or a board resolution say anything to the contrary, the notice can be written or oral and need not detail an agenda for the meeting.

That is the legal position, but there is a clear contrast here with what today would be regarded as best practice. As chapter 3 describes, the Combined Code for listed companies says that boards should meet regularly, there should be a schedule of matters that may only be settled by the board, and directors should be properly briefed. (The ICSA website has further guidance on this.) The Code now requires that the directors' annual report contains a record of attendance at board and committee meetings.

The articles will usually stipulate a minimum number of directors to form a quorum before the meeting can go ahead. But it is important to realise that:

- having a quorum is not a substitute for giving notice of a meeting. Achieving a quorum will not validate a board meeting if reasonable notice has not first been given to all directors;

- when calculating the quorum, the articles will often exclude any director who cannot vote on a particular resolution, perhaps because they have an interest in a contract under consideration.

Votes at a board meeting will be calculated on the basis of one for each director present, with the chairman having a casting vote in the event of a tie, unless the articles provide for anything different. A director with a personal interest in a matter that is the subject of the vote will usually be excluded from voting, but the articles need to be checked on the point (see section 2 of chapter 7).

In the case of larger companies, if the articles are well drafted, board meetings by telephone or video conference will be permitted. And for smaller companies, board resolutions may often be in writing, signed by all the directors entitled to receive notice.

Where a meeting is held, there is a legal requirement that minutes are taken (and the Companies Act 2006 requires them to be retained for at least 10 years). Minutes allow a director to have their views on a matter recorded – something that can be useful if questions are raised in the future, particularly after an insolvency (see section 3 of chapter 8).

The board can delegate matters to sub-committees, and listed companies are now required by the Combined Code to have audit, remuneration and nomination committees. Resolutions establishing committees may dictate quorum, notice and other requirements; failing that, they will follow the same rules as for the full board.

Annual General Meeting

A public company must hold an annual general meeting once each calendar year, and there must not be more than 15 months between each AGM.

The time and place of the AGM are matters for the board to decide but, given that the AGM is a rare opportunity for shareholders to have their say and to question directors publicly, companies have faced criticism when they have opted for times and venues that make it difficult for many shareholders to attend.

Under the Companies Act 2006, a private company does not have to hold an AGM, though it can if it wants.

The Combined Code states that the chairmen of the board's audit, remuneration and nomination committees should be sure to attend the meeting so that they can answer relevant questions from shareholders. Shareholder attendance at AGMs is, however, usually very low, with many choosing to vote by proxy on the standard resolutions to be proposed, or not to vote at all.

Periodic furore at directors' pay packages, and the requirement that the directors' remuneration report be put to shareholders for approval, may, however, lead to increased numbers at AGMs, and some consequent flexing of shareholders' muscles.

The main purpose of most AGMs is for the directors "to lay before the company in general meeting" the previous year's audited accounts and accompanying reports. Note the wording here – there is no requirement that shareholders approve the accounts or accept them. Shareholders have no ability to reject the accounts. They must stand as they are, having been prepared by the directors and audited by the auditors. The AGM simply provides the opportunity for the directors to present the accounts; the resolution put to shareholders will usually be "to receive" the accounts and reports.

Apart from the accounts, usual business at the AGM will comprise the declaration of any dividend proposed by the board, the appointment of auditors and the fixing of their fees (the latter task usually being delegated to the board), and the election of any directors who are retiring because the articles say they must (see section on directors, above).

Listed companies will also commonly propose resolutions at the AGM to:

- ☐ give directors authority to allot shares, up to a certain limit;
- ☐ disapply pre-emption rights on the issue of shares, up to a certain limit;
- ☐ renew authority for the company to buy up to 10 per cent of its own shares;
- ☐ approve the directors' remuneration report.

The AGM is not restricted to this business and, in addition, will often be used to put to shareholders resolutions to amend the articles, adopt new share schemes or do anything else that requires their approval.

Shareholders can propose their own resolutions for an AGM but they have to act in sufficient numbers: there must either be at least 100 of them holding a certain amount of paid up share capital, or enough of them to represent at least five per cent of the votes.

Extraordinary General Meeting

If something requires shareholder approval and cannot wait until the next AGM, an Extraordinary General Meeting (EGM) will be called. Usually, it will be the directors who convene an EGM, but the shareholders can force the directors to hold an EGM if they collectively own at least one-tenth of the paid up voting share capital. If the board then fails to comply within 21 days, shareholders can go ahead and call the meeting themselves.

As with AGMs, the directors must act in good faith when convening an EGM and should avoid picking a time and place with the intention of making it difficult for shareholders to attend.

Notice

All shareholders are entitled to receive written notice of a meeting unless the articles say otherwise (a smaller company's articles may often state that notice is only to be given to those shareholders who have provided a UK address to the company). In addition, notice of a general meeting must also be given to each director (whether a shareholder or not) and to the auditors – a point that can often be missed.

The articles will state how notice can be given to shareholders, and it is important that their provisions are followed: failure to do so can invalidate the notice, the meeting and the resolutions passed at it.

Legislation introduced in 2000 allows notices to be sent electronically (by e-mail or fax) if a shareholder is in agreement. Since January 2007, a company has also been able to use a website.

Documents and information to be sent to shareholders can be posted on a website if a shareholder resolution allowing this has been passed (or the articles permit it). Shareholders can opt out and still require hard copies through the post. In any event, each time a document is put on the website shareholders must be told, usually by hard copy letter.

Where a notice is sent through the mail, the articles will stipulate first or second class post and when the notice is deemed given, usually 48 hours after posting. An AGM for a public company requires 21 clear days' notice; all other meetings – a private company AGM (if held) and all EGMs – only need 14 clear days. For these purposes, "clear days" means exclusive of the day on which the notice is deemed served and the day of the meeting.

An example will explain the way this works: a plc AGM notice may be posted on July 1. If the articles state that notices sent by post are served 48 hours later (excluding weekends and bank holidays), notice will be deemed given on July 3. Day 1 of the notice period will then be July 4; day 21 will be July 24, which means that the meeting can be held on July 25.

Note that the 14 and 21 day time limits apply from October 2007, unless a company's articles require longer notice. Before that date, all AGMs require 21 clear days, as do all special resolutions.

For listed companies, the Combined Code requires the AGM notice and related papers to be sent to shareholders at least 20 working days before the meeting.

The notice must give sufficient indication of the business of the meeting, so that a shareholder can decide whether to attend or not. This will usually be achieved by setting out in full the resolutions to be proposed at the meeting; and with special resolutions, it is a requirement that their full text is given, and no amendment of substance is made. The notice must also tell shareholders that they can appoint a proxy to attend and vote in their place at the meeting.

These notice periods can be dispensed with if, in the case of a private company, agreement is given by those holding at least 90 per cent of the nominal value of the voting shares. For a public company, that figure goes up to 95 per cent, though a plc's AGM always has to be called on full notice.

Special notice

In two specific situations "special notice" may be required:

- [ ] removing an auditor and appointing an auditor where there has been a change since the last AGM;
- [ ] removing a director.

Special notice is a commonly misunderstood concept. **Special notice is not given by the company, but to the company by a shareholder.**

Notice to move the relevant resolution must be given to the company at least 28 days before the meeting. Having received the special notice, the company must inform shareholders of the resolution when it gives notice of the meeting.

Shareholder circulars

Anything other than the routine AGM resolutions is likely to require some form of explanation to shareholders by the board in the form of a letter or circular. In the case of a listed company, the Listing Rules contain requirements for such a circular. For example, the directors must say whether they believe the proposal is in the best interests of shareholders as a whole, and they must recommend which way shareholders should vote.

Unless the circular is dealing with standard business of the type described in the Listing Rules, it must be submitted to the UK Listing Authority for approval before it is sent to shareholders.

Resolutions

There are four types of resolution, each with a different purpose and distinct requirements:

- **ordinary** – unless companies legislation or the articles require anything different, an ordinary resolution will be sufficient for all decisions to be taken by general meetings of shareholders. If proposed at a plc AGM, 21 clear days' notice will be necessary; if proposed at a private company AGM or at any EGM, only 14 clear days are needed (these limits are effective from October 2007, subject to the company's articles).

  An ordinary resolution will be passed if a simple majority of those shareholders who are present and vote are in favour. If a poll is called, it needs a simple majority of all the votes cast (one share giving one vote, unless the articles say differently).

  Note: it is a simple majority of those who vote, not of all shareholders – or even of all who attend the meeting.

- **special** – matters that are less routine and of more importance, such as changes to the articles of a company, a change of name or a switch from being a private to a public company, or vice versa, will require a special resolution. Unless proposed at a public company AGM, 14 clear days' notice of the resolution must be given (prior to October 2007, 21 clear days are needed). The notice must clearly state that a special resolution is to be proposed and it needs the support of 75 per cent of those voting or, on a poll, 75 per cent of the votes cast.

- **written** – historically, it has been possible for many resolutions of the members of a private company to be passed without a meeting provided **all** the shareholders who would otherwise be entitled to vote sign a written copy (not necessarily the same piece of paper, just the same wording).

  The Companies Act 2006 relaxes this rule so that only shareholders with more than 50 per cent of a private company's shares have to agree an ordinary resolution; for a special resolution, the figure goes up to 75 per cent. The resolution must still be circulated to all shareholders (it is a criminal offence not to do so) but there is no need to get a signature if a shareholder's agreement is signified in writing in some other way, such as an e-mail.

  This change, effective from October 2007, allows much greater use of written resolutions and means there will be little reason ever to hold a shareholder meeting for a private company.

Shareholders do not have to wait for the directors to propose a resolution: those holding at least five per cent of the votes can require the company to circulate their own resolutions. Any resolution circulated to the shareholders will lapse if it has not been agreed to by the necessary majority within 28 days.

Note that written resolutions still cannot be used by public companies.

6. Shares and share issues

A lot has been said already about shareholders, but little about the shares they hold.

Share capital

Historically, companies have had two kinds of share capital:

Authorised is the share capital the company has created and the maximum it can issue. A company with a £1m authorised share capital may, for example, have 10 million authorised shares of 10p each.

Issued is the share capital issued and held by shareholders. It may be all 10 million shares in the above example, or only nine million, leaving one million authorised but unissued.

From October 2008, however, the Companies Act 2006 does away with the requirement for authorised share capital, leaving just the shares that have actually been issued.

Share values

A share will have a **nominal or par value**: 1p, 10p, £1 or any other sum in any currency. And it is an absolute rule that a share cannot be issued fully paid for anything less than its nominal value – that is, it cannot be issued at a discount. A company cannot issue a £1 share fully paid for 99p or less. A company thus has no ability to issue free shares (but it may buy shares in the market and give them as free shares to employees, say, as part of an incentive scheme).

A company is able to issue shares **nil or partly paid**. That means it can issue a £1 share nil paid and take no money for it on issue; or it may issue the share partly paid, say as to 25p. The amount unpaid (the full £1 or the balance of 75p) remains due and will have to be paid when the company calls for payment at a time anticipated in the terms of the share's issue, or on a winding up if the company's assets are not enough to settle its liabilities.

Of course, a £1 share will often be issued with a price being paid to the company well in excess of that sum; the difference between the nominal value and the price paid is the premium. The directors are under a duty in issuing shares (as in all things) to act in the best interests of the company, and if a £1 share has a market value of £1.50, they must have a good reason for issuing it for anything less than £1.50. **The nominal value is only the minimum price at which shares can be issued.**

Different classes of share

Unless the articles say otherwise, all shares will rank equally. But to the extent they are given different rights – to dividends, to a return of capital on winding up and on voting – they will comprise different classes of share. A company may have one class of share or it may have many.

Ordinary shares are the basic building block of a company's share capital. They will carry votes (usually one each), have a right to a dividend if the directors decide to pay one, and also be entitled to share in any surplus on a winding up of the company. Other shares will take their rights, or lack of them, by reference to this base position. **Non-voting shares** are self-explanatory (and a rarity these days, generally shunned by investing institutions but favoured by companies with a substantial family shareholding – for example, Daily Mail and General Trust). **Preference shares** may have a preferential right to a dividend ahead of the ordinary shares, or to a return of capital, or both. **Deferred shares** will rank behind the ordinaries (and tend to be used in a capital reorganisation where there is a need to make the shares virtually valueless).

Where these different classes of share exist, the rights of each one can only be changed in line with requirements in the articles or, if they are silent, requirements in the Companies Act. The articles will commonly stipulate a certain level of consent to any change; in default, the Act requires the holders of 75 per cent in nominal value to consent in writing, or holders of shares of that class to pass a special resolution (see above) approving the change at a separate meeting. Outside investors in a non-listed company may often expand the definition of what amounts to a class right and so prevent certain acts of the company (for example, the payment of a dividend) without their prior consent.

Share issues

Directors cannot issue newly created shares without shareholder authority to do so. Two provisions of the Companies Act 1985 are key here and will be familiar from any listed company AGM notice:

☐   **section 80** stops the directors from issuing shares to anyone unless they are authorised to do so in the articles or by shareholders passing an ordinary resolution. This ban includes an agreement to issue shares and the grant of options that will result in a future issue of shares (although employee share schemes are exempt). Listed companies will ask shareholders to give them this authority each year at the AGM, but will have to respect certain limitations stipulated by institutional shareholders – the rule has been that only 15 per cent of the authorised share capital can be issued – and the authority has to be renewed at each AGM.

The Companies Act 2006 replaces this in October 2008 with new sections 549 and 551, and the restriction will no longer apply to a private company with only one class of share.

☐   **section 89** obliges a company to offer new shares first of all to its existing shareholders in the same proportions they already hold shares. In other words, it upholds shareholders' right to be protected from dilution. If they are willing to pay the price asked for the new shares, they can have them. But this only applies where the shares are offered for cash – if a company is issuing shares in exchange for shares in another company, say, or in payment for a non-cash asset, there is no requirement to offer the shares to existing shareholders first of all.

The section can be disapplied, along with section 80, either in the articles or by a shareholder vote, though only by a special resolution. These rules are repeated in the Companies Act 2006 (section 561 and following).

Again, institutional shareholders have their price: only shares equal to five per cent of the issued share capital can be issued without first offering them to shareholders.

Rights issues and bonus issues

A **rights issue** is a common way for a company to raise fresh capital: it issues new shares, offering them first to its existing shareholders. Indeed, section 89, discussed above, obliges a company to treat any issue of shares for cash as a rights issue unless the shareholders have first agreed otherwise. (A rights issue for a listed company will often not follow the section 89 procedure because of various practical difficulties and the additional requirements of the Listing Rules.)

A listed company rights issue will usually offer shares at a discount to the current market price, sometimes a heavy discount if the shareholders' appetite for the shares needs to be stimulated. That discount means that there is an inherent value in the right to be offered the shares, and the shareholders in a listed company can trade those rights and realise that value if they do not want to take up the shares themselves.

Alternatives to a rights issue include an **open offer** where shareholders are invited to subscribe for a number of new shares based on their proportionate entitlements. This can be less complex than a rights issue but it does not give shareholders the opportunity to trade their rights to take up shares and so benefit from the discount. A **vendor placing** may also be used where a company is buying shares in another. Shares are allotted by the purchaser to the sellers of the target but the purchaser's investment bank agrees to find investors or placees who will take those shares and so give the sellers cash. Institutional shareholders of the purchaser may insist on a clawback whereby those shares are first offered to them in proportion to their existing holdings.

A **bonus issue** involves no new money. Also called a **capitalisation or scrip issue**, it takes a sum from the company's reserves (distributable profits that could be used to pay a dividend, or the share premium account) and capitalises it by using it to pay for the new shares. The issued share capital is increased without any new money being invested. The new shares are issued to existing shareholders pro rata to their shareholdings and so no dilution occurs.

duties

CHAPTER 2

1.   Introduction

It must be admitted that directors' legal duties are onerous and the penalties for breaching them can be stiff (see section 8 below). But it is important to remember that there is no expectation of perfection or infallibility. The overriding legal requirement is to act honestly, competently and conscientiously.

Provided directors have a proper understanding of their role and take basic protective measures, the risks of committing a breach of duty can be kept to an acceptable level.

In this chapter, we explain some of the legal duties owed by a director and examine the code of directors' duties in the Companies Act 2006.

2.   The nature of a director's relationship with the company and the shareholders

Many of the duties imposed under the law arise because the director acts as a fiduciary for the shareholders of the company. A fiduciary is someone who exercises powers or holds money or assets on behalf of others. Thus, the trustee of a family trust is a fiduciary for the beneficiaries; a solicitor holding money for a client is a fiduciary for that client.

The law and the judges provide protection for those on whose behalf fiduciaries act.

Directors should always see themselves as custodians of the company: its assets are not theirs to deal with solely as they wish.

3.   The extent of a director's power and authority

Directors do not have unlimited powers to run a company on behalf of the shareholders. They may only exercise the powers granted to them either by the general law or by the company's constitution (the articles of association – see chapter 1, section 3). For that reason, most companies will have an article on the lines of: "the directors are responsible for the management of the company's business, for which purpose they may exercise all the powers of the company".

Unless specific powers and authority have been delegated to a named director, it will usually be the case that powers can only be exercised by the board of directors acting together as a body.

4. Types of director

Does the law differentiate between types of director? Not as much as the layman might imagine. Individuals can perform significantly different roles but still have the same (or similar) legal accountability, as can be seen below.

Executive directors

An executive director is a director who is also an employee of the company. Their contract of employment will impose specific duties: for example, a finance director will be responsible for the day to day management of the company's finances.

Non-executive directors

Non-executive directors, by contrast, are not employees of the company. They will usually have a non-executive appointment letter rather than a contract of employment. That means they are paid fees, not salaries (see chapter 3 for more on their role). They will usually be part-time and will not be expected to be involved in the day to day running of the company.

Despite this, **there is no legal distinction between executive and non-executive directors.** Many of the duties placed on them will be the same.

Shadow directors

Shadow directors are those who, while not having formal titles or appointments, act as if they are directors and have a history of influencing the board (see chapter 1, section 4).

CORPORATE DIRECTORS: THE 2006 RULES

A director does not have to be an individual. A company can serve as a director on the board of another company. The use of "corporate directors" is, however, curtailed under the Companies Act 2006, which requires every company to have at least one individual or, in legal parlance, "natural person" on the board from October 2008.

Corporate directors can be represented at board meetings by different people at different times. They can also be used to distance individuals from liability. But with the Act requiring at least one individual as a director, there will always be one person of flesh and blood on the board who is **personally accountable for its failings.**

A shadow director may be held equally liable with the formally appointed directors for the consequences of an insolvency (see chapter 8).

The safest course is to assume that if you are a director of a company or act (in the eyes of the law) as if you are, you will be personally accountable when things go wrong.

5.   Prohibitions on acting as a director

The Companies Act 2006 excludes the following from being directors:

- undischarged bankrupts;
- people disqualified under the Company Director's Disqualification Act 1986 (see 14, below);
- people under 16 (this is a change to the law, effective October 2008).

Further restrictions may be imposed by the articles of association; it used, for example, to be common for the articles to require a director to hold shares in the company.

The 2006 Act removes the rule that directors of a public company have to go when they reach 70 unless the articles or shareholders say otherwise; from April 2007, there has been no upper age limit.

6.   Delegation of duties

Directors should be aware that when they delegate any of their duties to others, including the company secretary (see chapter 1, section 4), the responsibility and liability for fulfilling those duties remains with them.

The directors should periodically satisfy themselves that the secretary or other delegate is carrying out his or her tasks properly and that all legal requirements are being met. Any warning signs to the contrary should be followed up.

7.   The code of directors' duties

When the Department of Trade and Industry began the task of drafting a Companies Act for the 21st century (see the box in chapter 1), the law on directors' duties must have seemed an obvious candidate for reform. Built up since the 19th century by judges deciding different cases, it was in places uncertain, contradictory and anachronistic.

The code of directors' duties, contained in the Act and effective from October 2007, is the government's solution to the problem. This streamlines and clarifies the old rules and as such can be seen as a welcome development. It's important, however, to realise that it is more than a consolidation or simplification of what's gone before. The DTI has introduced a new concept, **"Enlightened Shareholder Value"**, and changed the rules.

The old formula was clear that a director's primary duties were to the company and its shareholders. There was a subsidiary duty to employees, and creditors always took precedence on insolvency, but the law was settled that a director should act in the best interests of all shareholders, including future shareholders. Now, enlightened shareholder value requires directors to consider other interests that may affect a company's success. A varied group of stakeholders has to be taken into account as well as shareholders.

The code of directors' duties applies to all companies, public and private, holding and subsidiary (and is not to be confused with the Combined Code on Corporate Governance, which applies only to listed companies – see chapter 3). It is a statutory benchmark of best practice for all.

What follows in this section explains the new rules. Companies and their directors will be well advised to take account of them from an early date.

Duty to act within your powers

As we have seen, directors have the job of managing the company and they are given certain powers to enable them to do that. But they must act according to the company's constitution and use those powers in the interests of the company, not to further their own narrow interests. So, for example, their power to issue new shares must be used for the purpose of raising capital for the business. Issuing shares to your cronies just to keep voting control in friendly hands is an abuse of power and a breach of duty.

Duty to promote the success of the company

This is a new duty, a re-casting of the old law that imposed a duty to act in good faith in the best interests of the company as a whole. The language is now subtly different; a director of a company must act in the way they consider, in good faith, would be most likely to **promote the success of the company for the benefit of its members as a whole.**

RESPONSIBLE BUSINESS BEHAVIOUR

The six factors that boards cannot ignore

As part of its decision-making process, a board needs to consider the following factors and weigh up their influence on its overriding **duty to promote the company's success**.

Of course, some of the six factors will be more relevant than others; much depends on the type of decision being made. There is no requirement to waste time considering the environment and your suppliers where they are clearly unconnected to the matter at hand.

By the same token, some decisions will require the board to have "regard to" other things as well. The list is not exclusive; it is a prompt, a guide for the "thinking" board.

☐ **the likely long-term consequences of any decision.** Promoting a long-term investment culture was a key objective of the government in introducing the Companies Act 2006 (see chapter 1). Some companies may find themselves with share registers made up entirely of hedge funds and active value investors who look only for short-term returns. Despite that, the relevance of the long view is something a board is required to consider.

☐ **the interests of employees.** Directors have been required to pay regard to employees' interests for many years but it has seldom raised much concern because employees have no direct means of enforcing this duty. That continues to be the case. Of course, employees may not have common interests. In the unhappy circumstances where the directors have to choose between shutting factory A or factory B, the legislation gives them no help in deciding between one group of employees and another.

☐ **the need to foster business relationships with suppliers, customers and others.** This may seem a statement of the obvious; it's a poor company indeed that's not aware of the importance of this. Nonetheless, small suppliers of large supermarkets may be one group that welcomes the statutory requirement.

☐ **the impact of the company's operations on the community and the environment.** Few large companies now feel they can ignore the environment (see the story of Shell's Brent Spar episode in the box on page 34), but the "community" is perhaps a trickier concept. The issue may be obvious where one company dominates a town and provides much of the employment and local wealth, but it may not be so clear cut where the interests of one community conflict with another.

☐ **the desirability of maintaining a reputation for high standards of business conduct.** Corporate buccaneers, in other words, have to think twice. (Whether this requirement will stop them is, of course, another matter.)

☐ **the need to act fairly between members.** This is old law, but remains good. The private shareholder with a few hundred shares is entitled to the same treatment as the institution with many millions of shares. The disclosure obligations of listed companies make the same point on the dissemination of inside information (see chapter 9).

(All this becomes irrelevant when a company is insolvent. Then the interests of creditors take precedence over all else – see chapter 8.)

DECISION TAKING AND RECORD KEEPING: DIRECTORS' SELF-DEFENCE

The requirement under the code of duties to pay regard to six specific factors of responsible business behaviour (see the box on page 32) inevitably raised the possibility of more paper work. If the law required directors to have regard to these six factors in reaching their decisions, and threatened consequences for them if they did not (see section 8), then lawyers were surely going to advise boards to keep detailed records of their compliance, weren't they?

The government, which promoted the Companies Act 2006 as a way of cutting red tape, was keen to play down the idea. The attorney general tried to reassure: "There is nothing in this Bill that says there is a need for a paper trail … I do not agree … that directors will be subject to a breach if they cannot demonstrate that they have considered every element."

Nonetheless, the question of how directors were going to defend themselves against allegations that they had ignored, say, the interests of employees or the community, remained "live".

An attempt at an answer was made by the GC100, a group of in-house lawyers and company secretaries at FTSE 100 companies. They argued that best practice should be for management to prepare a background paper when a board is asked to make a decision of any importance. That paper will deal with all relevant factors (it can ignore any that are not relevant). It is then for the directors to read their briefing papers and to use their judgment in arriving at a decision.

That seems a sensible solution. Minutes do not need to reprise a lengthy boardroom debate weighing up competing factors. The proper place for a consideration of those issues is the board paper circulated ahead of the meeting. That will be good evidence that the directors have complied with their duty to consider all relevant factors.

Lawyers may worry about how you define "success", but the intention behind the "new" duty seems to be on the same lines as the old. There is, though, one important new element. This can be seen from the DTI's commentary on the new wording: "this duty, which codifies the current law, enshrines in statute what is commonly referred to as the principle of **Enlightened Shareholder Value**".

Effectively, the Companies Act introduces on to the statute book for the first time the concept of the "stakeholder" – that is, someone other than a shareholder who has an indirect interest in what a company may be doing. The duty to promote the success of the company is not simply a codification of an old law, but the introduction of a new one.

THE CODE OF DIRECTORS' DUTIES – HOW IT MAY WORK IN PRACTICE

In many ways, the code of directors' duties does little more than enshrine in law what many directors have known for years: that the success of the company has to be seen in the round; that it's not enough to think only of short-term gain or immediate commercial interests. Two examples illustrate the point.

Manchester United

In 2005 Malcolm Glazer was close to succeeding in his bid for Manchester United. But although his offer of 300p a share was generally held to be fair, the board held off from advising shareholders to accept. Having looked at the Glazer business plan and his method of financing the bid with many millions of debt, they concluded that a takeover on those terms would place a "significant financial strain on the business", and that that was not in the company's best interests.

Shareholders are free to act in their own financial interests and most takeovers are decided in favour of the highest bid. But here the board looked beyond the current shareholders and focused instead on the interests of the company as a separate entity made up of future as well as current shareholders, and of creditors and employees as well. A company over-burdened with debt was not in their interests. In a foreshadowing of the Companies Act 2006, the board preferred the long-term consequences for the company over the short-term benefit for shareholders.

Shell

In 1995 Shell decommissioned its Brent Spar oil storage installation in the North Sea. It had no more use for it and, having taken expert advice, decided that the best solution was to tow it out to the mid-Atlantic and sink it.

Public outrage ensued. Greenpeace occupied the Spar, 50 Shell service stations in Germany were damaged by protesters, two were fire-bombed and the German Chancellor made a formal protest to the British prime minister.

As it saw its carefully nurtured reputation begin to shatter, Shell was forced to re-think. It halted the disposal, revised the plan and came up with an alternative – the offending hulk was recycled as the base for a roll-on/roll-off ferry quay at Mekjarvik in Norway.

Although the original disposal plan seemed to be the best option for Shell looked at in narrow commercial terms, that was not enough. The company had to realise that a rigorous assessment of the environmental, social and health impact of any major project was equally necessary for its long-term success.

To fulfil this duty, the legislation says that directors must have regard to six factors that demonstrate what the DTI calls "responsible business behaviour" in reaching their decisions. (See the box on page 32.)

Note the wording here. "Have regard to" is key. There is no requirement that any one factor is given precedence over another, that employees must be favoured over the environment, for example, or the community over customers. The final decision might ignore all six factors – but the board needs to be able to demonstrate that it has at least thought about them.

In practice, then, the new law may not represent a huge change. The success of the company remains the paramount concern for directors. The legislation prompts the board to think about these different factors, but they must remain subsidiary to the over-arching requirement the directors have to act in the way they believe, in good faith, is most likely to promote the company's success. (Where a company is set up for other purposes than to benefit its shareholders – where it's a charity, for example – you can substitute that other purpose.)

The new law does, however, have implications for decision taking and record keeping, and these are examined briefly in the box on page 33. But for many companies the concept of enlightened shareholder value is nothing revolutionary; they have been thinking about these factors, or something like them, for years. The duty merely gives statutory force to something that responsible boards of directors should be doing anyway.

Duty to exercise independent judgment

A director is on the board to act in the best interests of the company as a whole, not to represent the interests of just one shareholder or even a group of like minded investors. That rule applies irrespective of the circumstances in which the director has been appointed.

In a company set up as a joint venture between two businesses, each shareholder will commonly have the right to appoint an equal number of directors. Similarly, a private equity investor will commonly put a director on the board to safeguard its investment. But in each case those directors risk trouble if they are seen to act only in the narrow interests of the shareholder who appointed them. Their duty is to the company as a whole and to all the shareholders in the company. A director must not be a "plant" or a partisan.

Duty to exercise reasonable care, skill and diligence

The law requires a director to use reasonable care, skill and diligence in carrying out their tasks.

What does this mean in terms of the standards expected of a director? At the most basic level, that you must work at it: directorship is not a sinecure or an honorary position; it's a "proper" job, requiring "reasonable diligence".

Then there is a double test. First, there is an objective standard: a board member must have the knowledge, skill and experience that would reasonably be expected of someone doing that job. Second, a subjective standard must also be met: a director has to perform according to the knowledge, skill and experience they actually have.

So there is a basic level of competence that will be expected from all a board's members; but there is also a higher standard expected of those with some special skill or experience. A qualified accountant doing the job of finance director will be judged against the standard of a fellow professional closely following the detail of the company's finances; if they have particular knowledge or experience, they will be judged by that higher standard as well.

A non-executive director may not have the detailed knowledge of the company's business and will not see all of the information available to management, but they will have a broader experience and therefore will be expected to use that to probe and challenge. Just like executive directors, they will also be expected to bring relevant professional skills and qualifications to bear. When questions were raised over the financial shenanigans at Enron, much was made of the fact that Lord Wakeham, a non-executive director who sat on the company's audit committee, was a chartered accountant.

Duties relating to conflicts of interest

Directors' obligations to the company must not clash with obligations they owe (or feel they owe) to others; directors must be incorruptible. These are the principles behind the following three statutory duties:

- ☐   a general duty to avoid a conflict of interest;
- ☐   a duty not to accept benefits from third parties;
- ☐   a duty to declare an interest the director may have in a proposed transaction or arrangement with the company.

We examine these more closely in chapter 7 – together with a related duty in respect of existing transactions.

8. Remedies where there is a breach

If a director breaches any of the duties described above, what are the consequences?

Claims by the company

The company itself can bring a claim against the erring director if it can show that it has suffered some loss. If the director has made some personal profit, they can be required to surrender the gain to the company.

A contract or other arrangement entered into by the director in breach of a duty will be void, though it may be open to the company to ratify the agreement if it wishes to do so.

The company may also seek:

- ☐ an injunction to stop the director from carrying out or continuing with the breach;

- ☐ damages by way of compensation where the director has been negligent;

- ☐ restoration of the company's property;

- ☐ the rescinding of a contract in which the director had an undisclosed interest.

Claims by a company are often retrospective, brought by members of the existing board against their predecessors. (It is, after all, unlikely that a board will choose to sue itself; turkeys don't vote for Christmas.)

When Equitable Life's problems with guaranteed income policies were fully revealed, the newly installed directors voted to pursue the former directors for the losses the company had suffered. It was only after several years of crippling litigation, which pushed several of the defendants towards bankruptcy, that the company agreed to withdraw its claims.

When a company is sold, the new owners may appoint fresh directors and, if things go wrong, they may cast around for past breaches and the opportunity to hold the old directors to account.

Shareholder claims

Shareholders have no right to claim against a director for any loss they believe they may have suffered as a result of breach of duty. A director owes their duties direct to the company and only the company can complain of any breach. However much their shares may have dropped in price, shareholders cannot recover that loss of value from the directors they hold responsible.

But because few companies will bring a claim against one of their own directors, the law has over the years developed a mechanism for shareholders to seek redress. Shareholders can ask the court to be allowed to bring a claim against a director **in the name of the company**. The claim is initiated and run by shareholders, but it is brought in the company's name and to recover the company's loss.

Like directors' duties, this is an area of law built up by the courts over the past 150 years or so in an ad hoc way, with little clarity for today's company director. So again the government has taken the opportunity of the 2006 Companies Act to revise and codify the law. We look at this in more detail in chapter 7, and examine whether this restatement of the law is likely to lead to more aggressive litigation against directors in the future.

Claims by a liquidator or administrator

Following an insolvency, a liquidator or administrator will be under a duty to consider a claim where a breach of duty is discovered.

Dismissal

Whatever the circumstances, regardless of who is in the right and whether or not there has been a breach of duty, the shareholders have the ability in the Companies Act to remove a director by ordinary resolution. The articles might make it easier for the shareholders to sack a director, but they cannot make it more difficult or remove this statutory right.

The company will still have to pay out for any notice period agreed under the director's service contract.

Ratification

Even where a director's breach of duty is clear, the shareholders can ratify the breach by ordinary resolution (that is, a simple majority vote – see chapter 1, section 5). If the errant director is also a shareholder, they cannot vote in their own favour; neither can their family or others connected with them.

But connected parties can vote if all shareholders support the director – unanimity will cure the mischief.

Excusing liability

A director in breach of a duty may also be relieved of any liability if they can convince the court that they acted honestly and reasonably in all the circumstances. This might happen where a director acted in good faith on the advice of a lawyer or other professional, but where the advice proved to be wrong.

Directors need not wait for proceedings against them before seeking the court's protection. They can bring their own action for a court order to exempt them from liability.

9. Other statutory duties

A wide range of statutes imposes duties on directors, including those dealing with taxation, the environment and discrimination. We focus on health and safety and competition law in sections 11 and 13 below, but you do not have to stray beyond the Companies Act to find a variety of further duties. More than 200 involve offences directors can commit, with a variety of penalties applying to each. The majority are summary offences that are dealt with by a magistrate. Generally, the sanctions are fines and a criminal record but, in some cases, the penalty will be imprisonment.

These duties relate to two categories:

☐ administrative and compliance matters;

☐ restrictions and disclosure requirements.

The former includes the proper maintenance and retention of books and records, and the preparation and lodging of documents and returns with the Registrar of Companies etc. The latter includes the disclosure of interests in contracts and transactions, and provides for certain other "fair dealing" requirements – see chapter 7.

10. Liability for directors' reports etc

It is worth looking in a little more detail at three areas where there is a mix of civil and criminal liability for what goes into a number of the reports directors are obliged to produce.

False or misleading statement in directors' reports

A director will be liable for any false or misleading statement in the annual directors' report and the directors' remuneration report (see page 74) or if they omit something from the reports that should have been included. But the director must have known the statement was wrong, or been reckless about it, or have been dishonest about leaving out the required information. This liability came into force under the Companies Act 2006 on January 20, 2007.

(Recklessness requires a conscious disregard as to whether the information was right or wrong.)

Even if knowledge or recklessness can be proved, the director's liability is only to the company, not to any outside investor; and the company has to show that it has suffered a loss as a result.

False or misleading statement in periodic financial information

Since November 8, 2006, there has also been a liability for the financial information in a company's annual and half year results and in the new interim management statements that provide a quarterly update. This derives from the EU's Transparency Directive and applies only to listed companies in the UK (not those on AIM or PLUS).

But this is not a personal liability for a director. If an investor acquires shares in a listed company and later incurs a loss because of something untrue or misleading in the company's results, or because of the omission of a material fact, it is the company that will have to pay compensation. And the liability only crystallises if a director knew that the information was untrue or misleading, or was reckless on the point, or they left out the required information with the intention to deceive.

So dishonesty or recklessness is needed on the part of a director, and honest mistakes should be excused.

Audit reports

It is a criminal offence for a director or company employee to give the auditors false or misleading information, or to fail to give them information they have asked for without delay. The first offence can lead to a two-year prison term; the second risks only a fine.

The Companies Act 2006 imposes a new obligation (effective April 2008) on directors: not to approve the company's accounts unless they are satisfied that they give a true and fair view of the financial position. In other words, they must not accept the opinion of the auditors automatically. They must formally ask themselves whether they agree that the accounts are "true and fair".

11. Health and safety duties

A company is responsible for ensuring the health and safety of its employees and customers and anyone else affected by its activities – "so far as is reasonably practicable". No employer is expected to provide total protection against all risks. Satisfying a court that you did everything reasonably practicable, however, can be difficult. Consequently, many employers choose to plead guilty rather than fight a health and safety case against them.

Breaches of health and safety law are criminal offences, and fines of £100,000 and more are increasingly common, with the Court of Appeal making it clear that the worst offending companies can expect penalties of up to £500,000. In 2007, Network Rail was fined £4m for "systemic and unacceptable" safety failures that led to the 1999 Paddington train crash. When seven people died in Barrow in Cumbria because of an outbreak of Legionnaires' disease, the local council was fined £125,000, and the judge was clear that if the accused had been a large company, the fine would have been in excess of a million pounds.

Although many prosecutions will result from accidents where employees and others have been harmed, the legislation does not require injury to have been caused before charges can be brought; merely exposing staff and customers to a hazard can be enough.

And it is not just the company that is at risk. **An individual director, company secretary or manager can be held criminally responsible if the company itself has been found guilty of an offence.**

The case against a director can be proved if the offence was:

☐ **committed with their consent** – they were aware of the circumstances and of the risks that caused the breach;

☐ **committed with their connivance** – they knew the risks but did not do anything about them;

☐ **attributable to their neglect** – they breached a duty of care they owed, without good reason.

A director who is found guilty is liable for fines and, in some cases, imprisonment. They can also be disqualified from acting as a director for up to two years and thus be deprived of some of their earning power.

Any fines they incur will not be covered under the terms of insurance policies (see chapter 7).

All this makes health and safety a significant area of risk for all companies and their directors. As such, it must be actively managed by the board – not left to a lowly official. The Combined Code on Corporate Governance and the Turnbull Guidance (see chapter 3, section 16) require listed companies to take account of health and safety when establishing and reviewing their systems of internal control.

The resources devoted to the management of health and safety risks should be commensurate with the seriousness of the issue and the size of the potential fines involved.

12.   Corporate manslaughter

At its worst, a breach of health and safety rules can result in death. The liability of a company and its directors for fatalities has been much in the news in the past 15 or so years, with tragedies such as the capsizing of the Herald of Free Enterprise, the King's Cross fire and various rail crashes raising the issue of corporate manslaughter and the related responsibility of both the company and individual directors.

Before a company can be convicted of manslaughter under current law, the prosecution must prove two things: first, that a single individual in the company is guilty of manslaughter; second, that this individual is the "controlling mind" of the company.

So if there is not enough evidence to convict an individual, there can be no prosecution of the company. Even where an individual is convicted, a large company can still find itself off the hook. Fatal accidents are often the result of failures by a number of people over a period of time. The larger the company, the greater the number; and the less likely the chance of proving that a single person was the "controlling mind".

In the past 15 years there have been just seven successful prosecutions of companies for work-related manslaughter. In each case, the convicted company has been a small organisation where it has been possible to identify one individual who had effective overall control.

This apparent bias towards larger companies has attracted widespread criticism, and successive promises of reform have been made. In March 2005, the government published a draft Corporate Manslaughter Bill, proposing a new offence of corporate manslaughter to apply to all corporate bodies. At the time of writing (March 2007), the Bill has still not become law.

The Bill moves the focus away from any one individual; instead, guilt arises if it can be proved that there was a failure of management at a senior level that:

- [ ] caused a person's death; and
- [ ] amounted to a gross breach of a relevant duty of care owed by the company to that person.

Other key points about the Bill are given below.

- [ ] Senior managers are defined as those who play a significant role in making decisions about the organisation as a whole, or at least a substantial part of it. So it is the actions or inactions of board members – and, perhaps, of managers just below board level – that will be examined, not the failings of relatively junior staff on the ground.

- [ ] To be deemed to have caused a death, a management failure must have made more than a minimal contribution to it. The required duty of care will exist between, for example, a company and its employees, and a company and its customers or those who use its goods and services.

- [ ] Gross breach means conduct that falls far below what can reasonably be expected in the circumstances.

- [ ] If a conviction is obtained, the company can be liable for an unlimited fine, and the court can make remedial orders forcing the company to put matters right. The parent company of a group may also be liable where the failure in a subsidiary is in fact a failure of the parent's senior managers.

- [ ] The new offence will only apply to acts or failures in the UK. There is no UK liability created for deaths caused overseas. And prosecutions will need the consent of the Director of Public Prosecutions – private proceedings will not be possible.

- [ ] The new offence will apply only to corporate bodies: there are no new proposals increasing the liability of directors themselves. This has proved controversial, with some arguing that the necessary change in culture will only come about when directors face a real threat of jail. One trade union has been quoted as saying: "Directors in the dock is what we want."

The Health and Safety Commission has published guidance on the responsibilities of directors. This can be downloaded from the Health and Safety Executive (HSE): www.hse.gov.uk/pubns/indg343.pdf

13. Competition law

Companies can face civil penalties of up to 10 per cent of global turnover if they infringe competition law and, since 2003, it has also been possible for directors in the UK to be held personally liable for serious breaches of EC and UK competition law. An individual who participates in a cartel can be found guilty of a criminal offence (the so-called "cartel offence") and a director of a company that commits any breach of competition law can also be disqualified from acting as a director for up to 15 years.

It is an offence punishable by up to five years' imprisonment or an unlimited fine (or both) for an individual dishonestly to agree to enter into or implement certain anti-competitive agreements in the UK. These include direct or indirect price fixing, the limiting of production or supply and market sharing or bid-rigging arrangements – i.e. the most serious "hard core" breaches of competition law.

What has to be proved for an individual to be held to be acting dishonestly? The court would apply a two-part test. First, was the individual acting dishonestly according to the standards of reasonable and honest people? Second, did they realise that what they were doing was dishonest by those standards?

The law also provides that a disqualification order (see 14, below) can be issued against a company director if they knew, or ought to have known, that the company had breached EC or UK competition law. This sanction applies to any breach – not just the "hard core" cartel infringements.

14. Disqualification

A defaulting director may expect not only personal or criminal liabilities as a consequence of a breach of duty but also a court order disqualifying them from acting as a director for up to 15 years.

A person can be disqualified from acting as a director on a number of grounds, including persistent breach of company law legislation and conviction for fraud. Most applications are made under the section of the Company Directors Disqualification Act that relates to a director of a company that becomes insolvent and to their "fitness" to be concerned in the management of a company.

If a disqualified director ignores the order, they will commit a criminal offence punishable by a prison sentence of up to two years.

15. Conclusion

Directorship carries significant responsibilities: to shareholders, employees, and in some cases, to creditors of the company. Under the 2006 Companies Act, a wider group of stakeholders must also be considered.

The law imposes duties on directors, and directors who breach them can be held personally liable. But the risks need to be kept in perspective. The law does not seek to penalise the innocent director. Directors can make mistakes – but they must not make them knowingly or dishonestly.

The legal and other professional costs of defending a director against claims can be very high. The company might not be able to offer ongoing financial support to a director faced with these costs. We look in detail at the area of directors' insurance and indemnities in chapter 7. But directors need to understand that having cover in place is not the end of the story: you need to know what the limitations on that cover are, and where you remain exposed.

corporate governance

CHAPTER 3

1. Introduction

Governance is a word that barely existed 20 years ago. Now it is in common use not just in companies but also in charities, universities, local authorities and National Health Trusts. It has become a shorthand for the way an organisation is run, with particular emphasis on its accountability, integrity and risk management.

The "revolution" started in the early 1990s with the **Cadbury Report** on the financial aspects of corporate governance, to which was attached a code of best practice. Aimed at listed companies and looking especially at standards of corporate behaviour and ethics, the "Cadbury Code" was gradually adopted by the City and the Stock Exchange as a benchmark of good boardroom practice. In 1995, the **Greenbury Report** added a set of principles on the remuneration of executive directors (in response to some particular "fat cat" scandals, notably that involving British Gas chief Cedric Brown, whose 75 per cent rise incensed both unions and small shareholders), and in 1998 the **Hampel Report** brought the two together and produced the first Combined Code. A year later, the **Turnbull Report** concentrated on risk management and internal controls.

In each case, the reports were prompted either by shareholder disquiet over perceived shortcomings in corporate structures and their ability to respond to poor performance, or to government threats of legislation if the corporate sector failed to put its house in order.

In 2002 Derek Higgs, an investment banker, was given the brief to look again at corporate governance and build on the previous reports to produce a single, comprehensive code. Shortly afterwards, the full consequences of the Enron and Worldcom scandals were realised, leading to new unease. The **Higgs Report** came out in early 2003, but was greeted with horror by some leading companies, with claims that it placed an unrealistic burden on non-executives and marginalised the role of the chairman. The task of taking Higgs's draft forward was passed to the Financial Reporting Council (FRC), a body established by government and comprising members from industry, commerce and the professions. The FRC consulted further and produced a revised Code that followed most of Higgs's recommendations but softened a few of the more contentious points, and so gained general acceptance. With rather less fuss, at the same time **Sir Robert Smith**, chairman of the Weir Group, was leading **a review of the role of audit committees** and his recommendations were incorporated into the new Code. The 2003 Code was updated with minor amendments in June 2006, with the new version applying to financial years beginning on or after November 1, 2006.

Is all this attention on governance good for business, in the hard, commercial sense? Views differ. Several surveys have claimed that companies with better corporate governance are more profitable; sceptics have countered that it is only the more profitable companies that can afford the time and effort to make sure they follow best practice. There is no doubt, however, that the demand of shareholders and other stakeholders for good governance is strong and continuing. Investors, unions, government and assorted pressure groups are all increasingly likely to condemn a business that fails to follow the "rules". The business case for good corporate governance is, therefore, not difficult to build.

This chapter concentrates on the main terms of the FRC's **Combined Code on Corporate Governance** of June 2006 – and on their implications for directors.

2. The reach of the Code

The FRC may be the custodian of the Code but compliance is a matter for the Listing Rules. Produced by the Financial Services Authority, these Rules regulate companies with a full listing on the London Stock Exchange.

The Code does not apply to:

☐ companies whose shares are traded on AIM or other markets not covered by the Listing Rules;

☐ a listed company incorporated outside the UK (though such companies do have a lesser reporting obligation).

There is, though, nothing to stop such companies complying with the Code if they choose to do so. Shareholder pressure, or simply a wish to conform with "best practice", may lead many "exempt" companies to follow some or all of the Code's recommendations. Most of the Code's principles, if not all the detailed provisions, provide a sound basis for the governance of many companies.

Indeed, the Code's reach increasingly extends beyond its immediate "target group" – what follows in this chapter may be of help to directors, trustees, governors and council members in many disparate organisations. The Code has been the impetus for the development of a more formalised approach to governance in other sectors. Universities have produced their own governance code; public sector bodies have guidance from the Independent Commission on Good Governance in Public Services. And mutual life companies are expected to follow guidelines on governance produced in the wake of the Equitable Life inquiry.

3.   The Code and the annual report

The Code is divided into "main principles", "supporting principles" and "provisions". The main principles are general statements of corporate life, which, at times, come close to motherhood and apple pie in their level of general acceptability. The first, for example, states: "Every company should be headed by an effective board, which is collectively responsible for the success of the company". Supporting principles expand on the main principles and give more guidance. But it is the Code's provisions that state the detailed requirements necessary, in the view of the Code's authors, to make sure the principles are upheld.

The Listing Rules seek to give the principles and provisions some force by placing two requirements on UK listed companies:

☐   the annual report and accounts must contain a statement explaining how the company has applied the main and supporting principles. (It is taken for granted that the principles are accepted; the only room for debate is over how they are applied.)

☐   the report and accounts must state whether the company has complied with the provisions throughout the year covered by the report. If the company has not complied with all of the provisions, or if it has complied with them for only part of the year, the departures must be listed and reasons for the non-compliance given.

4.   The comply or explain rule

This brings us to a key feature of the listed companies' Combined Code, copied to an extent by other codes derived from it: its regime of "comply or explain". UK listed companies must comply with the Code's detailed provisions or explain why they do not. Ignoring the Code is not an option; but if you have good reason to deviate from its terms, you may do so and leave it up to your members/shareholders to decide whether your reason is good enough. If you can talk to shareholders and demonstrate that departures from the Code's provisions are in the company's best interests, then non-compliance is unlikely to become a big issue.

Shareholders have no specific sanction if they disapprove of what you are doing, short of voting against the Directors' Remuneration Report if the debate is over boardroom pay, or voting one or more directors off the board – a somewhat extreme step. What they can do, though, is apply pressure with the aim of persuading the board to change its mind.

> ## MORRISONS: HOW SHAREHOLDERS CAN CHANGE GOVERNANCE
>
> A few years ago, the supermarket chain Morrisons seemed unencumbered by corporate governance principles. The company, led by the septuagenarian Sir Ken Morrison as full-time executive chairman, had no non-executive directors, no audit or remuneration committees and no shame in explaining that it did not think these were necessary. It was a FTSE 100 company and very much in the public eye. Institutional shareholders might not have liked its public defiance of generally accepted principles, but Morrisons was successful, and there was little they could do about it.
>
> Things began to change after Sir Ken decided to bid for rival chain Safeway in 2003. The chairman needed to raise money for the bid from shareholders, and one of the conditions they imposed was that he should at least appoint two non-executive directors. Over a year later and just before the AGM, two new non-executives duly appeared (though one resigned 10 months later). One institutional shareholder group commented, recognising the uphill task they still faced: "We welcome this step towards better corporate governance and hope to see formal board committees established in due course."
>
> Since then, further steps have been taken to make management structures "more satisfactory to the City". And following a number of profit warnings and acknowledged failures in its internal controls, the company now has a full complement of board committees manned by four independent non-executives (though they still do not equal in number the six executive directors).

As the case of the supermarket chain Morrisons shows, this can be most effective at those junctures when a company needs the support of its shareholders. (See box above.)

If the shareholders are not big enough or well organised enough to exert pressure or if they are unwilling to take the opportunities they have to do so, then the board can decide how much it complies. The key point is that the Code and its provisions are not compulsory; they are there for guidance and represent best practice.

5. The role of the board

The Code sets out its own view of the role of the board. This can be summarised as:

☐   providing entrepreneurial leadership;

☐   setting strategy;

☐   ensuring the human and financial resources are available to achieve objectives;

☐   reviewing management performance;

☐   setting the company's values and standards;

☐   satisfying itself as to the integrity of financial information and the robustness of financial controls and risk management.

The Code recognises that there are some issues that can only be decided by the board. It states that: "there should be a formal schedule of matters specifically reserved for its decision" and that the annual report should include a "high-level statement of which types of decisions are to be taken by the board and which are to be delegated to management". Guidance on drawing up a schedule of matters reserved for the board is available from the Institute of Chartered Secretaries and Administrators (ICSA) and from the IoD publication, *Standards for the Board.*

6. The chairman

The Code says the roles of chairman and chief executive should not be held by the same person.

"There should be a clear division of responsibilities at the head of the company between the running of the board and the executive responsibility for the running of the company's business. No one individual should have unfettered powers of decision" – *main principle A.2.*

This point met some strong vocal dissent when first made by Higgs but survived through to the FRC's Code. In practice, few large companies today have one individual fulfilling the roles of both chairman and chief executive. The chairman may not always be a part time non-executive: many are full time and describe themselves as executive chairman, but the roles of chairman and CEO are at least distinct. The former leads the board, ensures there is a good working relationship between the executive and non-executive directors and is primarily responsible for communications and liaison with shareholders. The Code also says the chairman must ensure that the rest of the board receives "accurate, timely and clear information" ahead of board meetings and other key decision points.

By contrast, the chief executive has responsibility for the day to day management of the company and putting into effect the decisions and policies of the board.

In those rare cases where one person does perform both roles, the board will need to explain to shareholders why it thinks that is right for the company. And, at the least, shareholders are likely to insist on a strong senior independent director (see 9, below) to counter-balance the joint chairman/CEO.

Equally to be frowned upon, according to the Code, is the previously widespread practice of a chief executive stepping up to become chairman of the same company. Higgs took the view that you could not have two popes in one company: a new chief executive was going to have a next to impossible job if his predecessor was still around as chairman, constantly looking over his shoulder and perhaps disagreeing with any departure from past policies. Defenders of the practice sang the praises of a chairman who often had years of experience with the company, still had much to offer and who was quite capable of establishing a good working relationship with a new CEO. Higgs's view prevailed, though the Code does concede that in exceptional cases the rule may be broken. Any board in breach should consult major shareholders in advance and set out its reasons for the appointment, both at the time and in the next annual report. Barclays Bank and, more recently, HSBC, have argued that only the incumbent CEO has the knowledge and experience of a large, multinational group's operations to fulfil the chairman's role.

GREENE KING: HOW THE BOARD CAN GET ITS WAY

In late 2004, the brewer and pub owner Greene King announced that its chairman was retiring and that, contrary to the Code's provisions, he was going to be succeeded by the chief executive. It advanced various reasons for this: the chief executive had made it clear he would not stay in his current role; the non-executives wanted both to retain his experience and skills and avoid losing its top two at the same time. Greene King had consulted its five largest shareholders, who collectively owned about 25 per cent of the company, and they were reported as being "supportive". (The fact that the board undertook to appoint two more independent directors, and that the company's share price had just hit a record high, no doubt helped.)

The Code says that a chairman should be independent at the time of their appointment. Put simply, this means having no "history", no previous relationships with the company (see section 7 of the main text). In theory, Greene King's new chairman failed the independence "test": he had held an executive position at the company and had long experience on the board. Nonetheless, the company went ahead with the appointment, arguing that the new chair made up for any lack of detachment by his "strength of character and *independent judgment*".

Consultation and explanation can make a real difference. This can be shown by the experience of Greene King – see the box on the previous page.

7. Independent non-executive directors

The Code makes a distinction between non-executives who are independent and non-executives who are not. To qualify for the former category, an individual must not only have the necessary independence of character and judgment but also be free of any connections that may lead to conflicts of interest.

The Code makes it clear that someone will not normally be considered independent if:

☐   they have been an employee of the group within the previous five years;

☐   they have a "material business relationship" with the company or have had one within the previous three years, including an indirect relationship as a partner, director, senior employee or shareholder of an adviser or major customer or supplier; (this would catch a partner from, for example, the company's audit firm moving on to the board after retirement);

☐   they receive remuneration from the company in addition to director's fees or they participate in the company's share option or performance related pay schemes or they are members of the pension scheme;

☐   they have close family ties with any of the company's advisers, directors or senior employees;

☐   they hold cross directorships or have significant links with other directors through involvement in other companies or bodies; (this works against the "old boys' club" method of appointing non-executives: George is finance director at company A and sits as a non-executive on the board of company B; Harry is chief executive at company B and sits as a non-executive at company A);

☐   they represent a significant shareholder;

☐   they have served on the board for more than nine years.

Ultimately, however, it is up to the board to decide who "qualifies". The board is expected to consider the above – and, indeed, any other factors that may impair independent judgment – but none of them is to be thought of as grounds for automatic "exclusion". It may be that an individual is judged to have the strength of character and integrity to remain unaffected by circumstances that, in theory, compromise their independence.

When they appoint non-executives, and each year when reporting to shareholders, the members of the board have to identify who is independent and who is not. If they have decided that, despite previous and/or current connections with the company etc, an individual may be classed as independent, they need to explain the reasons why.

Two examples will show the freedom boards have in practice – and the arguments that can be mustered against assumptions of non-independence:

☐ Sir Derek Higgs, author of the Higgs Report and the principal architect of the Code, was until 2006 a non-executive director of British Land. In addition, he served as a non-executive at Jones Lang LaSalle, who advise British Land on property matters. Despite this, the company was happy to state that it classed Sir Derek as an independent director because his other role at Jones Lang was not an executive position, he was not involved in any British Land related work there, and British Land paid less than one per cent of its turnover in fees to the firm. A similar justification was made in previous years in respect of Sir Derek's senior position at UBS Investment Bank, financial advisers and brokers to British Land.

☐ Pearson, publisher of the *Financial Times*, trumpeted in 2005 that it had two non-executives with a combined total of more than 30 years on the board, clearly in excess of the nine years a piece allowed by the Code. Both had continued to perform as "exceptional independent directors" and had "continued to demonstrate a robust independence and to make a substantial, constructively critical contribution as directors". Both eventually retired in 2006.

8. Composition and structure of the board

The Code states that:

"The board should include a balance of executive and non-executive directors (and in particular independent non-executive directors) such that no individual or small group of individuals can dominate the board's decision-taking" – *main principle A.3.*

The provisions supporting this say that at least half the board, not counting the chairman, should be independent non-executive directors. This means that a board of nine needs to have at least four independent non-executives to balance four executive directors, with the chairman being the ninth director. A board of eight that wants to comply with this guidance needs to have four independent non-executives, matching three executives and the chairman.

An exception is made for a "smaller company", defined as a company outside the FTSE 350 for the whole of the year before the year being reported on. Those smaller companies are urged to have at least two independent non-executive directors. (Indeed, they will need two if they are to comply with the Code's requirements for board committees – see 14, below.)

Again, these principles and provisions are for guidance only: a company is free to explain why it believes such numbers of independent non-executives are excessive or not right for its own particular circumstances.

The Code clearly gives a strong role to the non-executives. They should meet regularly, as a body, with the chairman, but without the executive directors; and at least once a year they should meet on their own under the leadership of the senior independent director (see below) to appraise the chairman's performance. They may outnumber their executive colleagues, whom they are expected **"to constructively challenge"**.

If the executive directors are interested in any matter that goes to the board, the non-executives may effectively be left in control. This situation is increasingly seen where a bid for the company is received from the management team, or from a private equity group with management involvement. The executives can play no part in the decision and it will be for the independent directors to decide alone whether to recommend the bid to shareholders.

What does all this mean for the structure of the board? Does it effectively create two tiers? The Code is keen to stress that it still believes in the **unitary board**. The non-executives are not meant to comprise a separate supervisory body on, for example, the German model. Executive and non-executive, independent and chairman are all members of the single decision-making board at the heart of a UK company.

9. The senior independent director

Where independent non-executive directors do sit on the board, one of them should be chosen as senior independent director. This creates an alternative point of contact for major shareholders who may have made little headway in discussions with the chairman, chief executive or finance director – or who may have concerns about the performance of such individuals. The senior independent director also takes the lead in annual appraisals of the chairman.

The post caused some controversy when first proposed by Higgs. It was argued that shareholders would be confused: should they talk to the chairman or the senior independent? And was there not a risk that, if they talked to both, different messages would be given – or a different spin given to the same facts? Also, chairmen saw the senior independents as muscling in on their patch. In practice, however, few problems have arisen. As long as care is taken over their selection, there seems no reason why the senior independent should not enjoy a good working relationship with the chairman.

10. Appointment of directors

According to main principle A.4, there should be **"a formal, rigorous and transparent procedure"** for the appointment of new directors. In other words, the days of putting your friends from the golf club on the board are over.

The Code gives the recruitment task to a nomination committee, a majority of whose members should be independent non-executive directors.

There is no ban on the chairman or the chief executive being a member – as is consistent with the committee's role in making recommendations for executive as well as non-executive appointments. The chairman may chair the committee – though they should stand aside when it comes to choosing their successor.

The committee is expected to:

☐ evaluate the balance of skills, knowledge and experience on the board and, in the light of that, draw up a description of the role it is seeking to fill and the capabilities required;

☐ use external search consultancies or open advertising in the hunt for candidates for the chairman's role and non-executive posts. (Failure to cast the net this wide must be explained in the annual report);

☐ make appointments only on merit and after assessing candidates by means of objective criteria;

☐ ensure that candidates for the chairmanship and non-executive roles will have the necessary time to devote to the company;

☐ set out the terms and conditions of the appointment of non-executive directors – including the expected time commitment – and make those terms publicly available.

Individuals who are non-executives in one company will often be executive directors in another – and vice versa. It is generally thought to be a good thing that an executive gets experience of the workings of another company and another industry. However, it is important that the demands on the individual are realistic – the Code says that the board should not agree to a full-time executive taking on more than one FTSE 100 company non-executive directorship or the chairmanship of such a company.

11. Induction and training for directors

The authors of the Code believe that new directors have to be properly trained. This means an effective induction process when the director joins the board and an on-going programme of professional development. In the words of main principle A.5, directors should **"regularly update and refresh their skills and knowledge"**. (If they do not they cannot possibly hope to keep up with the pace of legislative and regulatory change. The new code of directors' duties in the Companies Act 2006 – see chapter 2 – is only one recent development.)

"The company," says the Code, "should provide the necessary resources for developing and updating its directors' knowledge and capabilities". Note also the obligation in Listing Principle 1: **"A listed company must take reasonable steps to enable its directors to understand their responsibilities and obligations as directors."**

The essential point is that directors must be given the right "equipment" and get the right preparation to do their jobs/discharge their duties. There is reference to "tailored induction". Thus the Code recommends that new non-executives get the chance to meet major shareholders as part of their induction process (A.5.1) and that **"consideration should be given to visiting sites and meeting senior and middle management"** (Higgs Suggestions for Good Practice).

For all directors, the right "equipment" includes **"accurate, timely and clear information"**. The **company secretary**, under the direction of the chairman, must, say the supporting principles, ensure **"good information flows within the board and its committees and between senior management and non-executive directors"**.

The words "clear" and "good" here are sometimes forgotten when directors are first appointed. Companies can tend to overburden an individual. As ICSA says in its guidance notes on the induction process, "it has become apparent that some newly appointed directors have been completely overwhelmed with the sheer volume of documents and other papers provided by the well meaning company secretary to such an extent that some have been completely put off by it". To avoid this, ICSA suggests giving the director essential information only on their appointment and providing further necessary information in the subsequent few weeks. Subsidiary information can follow once the first two batches have been digested.

The company should also be prepared to pay for independent professional advice where the directors judge it necessary.

12. Performance evaluation

In the past few years, the idea of board-level appraisals has become increasingly accepted. Thus main principle A.6 is that **"the board should undertake a formal and rigorous annual evaluation of its own performance and that of its committees and individual directors"**.

As with any appraisal process, the intention is that strengths are recognised and built upon and weaknesses are addressed – which may mean, ultimately, asking a director to go. Questions to ask will include:

☐ is the director's contribution to the board an effective one?

☐ do they demonstrate commitment to the role?

☐ are they giving the job the time it requires?

Once a year, the board should look at itself and assess what it does, its failures and successes, and a similar process should be conducted by the board for each of its committees.

The annual report needs to explain how these appraisals are carried out. There is no guidance in the Code as to whether it can or should be done in-house, though many boards seem to be reporting the use of home-grown procedures based on one-to-one interviews between the chairman and each director. Most human resources departments will have experience of appraising employees, and some of the same principles will apply here. Equally, there may be merit in bringing in outside consultants to facilitate the appraisal process. Ultimately, however, it will be the responsibility of the board to draw conclusions from the process and to act upon them.

The chairman does not escape. His or her performance should be evaluated by the non-executives as a whole, under the leadership of the senior independent director. But they need to consult the executive directors and take account of their views.

13. Re-election

A poor appraisal may result in the chairman asking a director to stand down. That will be an internal board matter. But what of the shareholders? What power do they have to get rid of directors who, in their eyes at least, have under-performed? Shareholders can pass a resolution at a general meeting to remove a director if they can muster more than half the votes cast. But in many companies, the AGM also gives the shareholders the opportunity to vote on the re-appointment of some of the directors. Many company articles will provide that all new directors have to stand for re-election at the AGM following their appointment, and that is a provision echoed by the Code. Articles will commonly stipulate that a third of the directors should retire and stand for re-election each year. The Code expresses the same sentiment, but with a variation: each director (executive or non-executive) should be subject to re-appointment by the shareholders every three years.

Although shareholders have rarely used their power to remove directors in this way, three Manchester United directors were shown the red card at their 2004 AGM when American sports tycoon Malcolm Glazer, who later bid for the company, took his revenge on those coming up for re-election after he was refused access to the company's books. (Glazer owned 28.1 per cent of the club's shares.)

The shareholders may not be privy to the detail of the board's appraisal of individual directors but the Code does require the chairman to confirm to them that, following an appraisal, the performance of the director up for re-election **"continues to be effective and to demonstrate commitment to the role"**. Indeed, the board is required to tell shareholders why it believes an individual director should be re-elected.

The non-executive's letter of appointment needs to take account of the requirement that he or she stands for re-election every three years. The Code says that two three-year terms should be the norm and a third, making nine years in all, should be **"subject to particularly rigorous review"** and take account of the need for **"progressive refreshing of the board"**. Despite this, nine-year terms are very common, and some institutional shareholders now seem relaxed about them. Many companies would argue that there is little point in sacrificing a director's experience and knowledge of a group after only six years because of an unjustified fear that they may have gone stale. Once nine years are reached, the Code suggests that the director should be subject to annual re-election.

As we have seen in section 7, serving more than nine years raises the assumption of a lack of independence, which has to be rebutted each year by the board in the annual report.

14. Board committees

The Combined Code requires a board to have three committees: remuneration, audit and nomination.

All of these committees should have terms of reference, and these should be publicly available (usually on the company's website).

In each case, the terms should set out clearly what the committee is to do, stating whether it is to take decisions or merely make recommendations. A remuneration committee will, in accordance with the Code's provisions, commonly have delegated authority to set the executive directors' pay. Its proposals will be discussed with the chairman and/or chief executive, and there may be a broad policy on directors' pay agreed with the board, but the responsibility will lie with the committee not the board. By contrast, the nomination committee will usually merely make recommendations to the full board and leave the final decision to the board as a whole.

The 2003 Combined Code was clear that the audit and remuneration committees should be made up only of independent non-executive directors. Neither the chairman (whose independence is automatically assumed to be compromised after appointment) nor any executive director should be a member. The nomination committee, by contrast, just needed a majority of independent non-executives; the chairman and the chief executive could be members, so long as they were outnumbered by the independents. The 2006 amendment to the Code made an important change here: now chairmen may sit on their own remuneration committees so long as they were deemed to be independent immediately before their appointment to the chair. Nonetheless, it still remains the case that another director should act as chairman of the committee.

Nothing in the Code prevents executive directors, or indeed any other employee or outside adviser, being invited to attend a particular committee meeting. So the finance director may commonly sit in on audit committee meetings – the Code recognises that their presence will often be necessary and desirable. Likewise, the head of HR will often be needed at remuneration and nomination committee meetings. But neither has the right to attend or vote; they are only there by invitation.

The board may appoint further committees as necessary, either on a continuing basis to deal with on-going matters (for example, treasury or risk) or ad hoc to deal with a particular acquisition or matter of strategy. Many companies will have an executive committee made up of the chief executive and those who report directly to him or her but excluding the chairman and the non-executives. It may meet monthly or weekly and will have daily executive responsibility for the company's affairs.

15. Audit

The role of the audit committee is so important to good governance that it was subject to a separate review in 2003. The Smith Guidance on Audit Committees, produced by Sir Robert Smith, is annexed to the Code.

Composition of the committee

The Code provides that the audit committee should consist of at least three independent non-executive directors, or two if the company is outside the FTSE 350. And the board should "satisfy itself" that at least one of those independent non-executives has **recent and relevant financial experience**. The Code is not specific about what constitutes "relevant experience", but Smith says it means a professional qualification from one of the accountancy bodies. Note that Morrisons' new audit committee admitted to lacking the "recent and relevant financial experience" required by the Code and had to recruit an independent firm of accountants to advise it as a result.

Commonly, the "expert" may be a retired finance director from another company or perhaps a former partner of an accountancy firm. To comply with the Code's recommendations for independence the board should, of course, exclude its own former finance directors and auditors. In any event, it must justify its choice in the annual report.

Given the complexity of the issues usually faced by an audit committee, it is essential that its members are given proper induction and training.

Roles of the committee

The Code gives the audit committee four main roles.

- ☐ It is **the guardian of the integrity of a company's financial statements and performance**. It must, in short, be satisfied that all figures presented to shareholders and the outside world will stand up to scrutiny and can be relied upon. This requires committee members not only to understand the financial statements and how they are made up (no mean feat as accounting standards get ever more complicated), but also to quiz the finance director and the external auditors as draft accounts are produced. Like all good non-executives, they must ask the right questions and be persistent if a satisfactory and intelligible answer is not forthcoming.

- ☐ This general oversight of the company's accounts means that the audit committee also has a role in **checking the company's internal financial controls**, reviewing them and their operation and **ensuring that necessary risk management systems are in place**. Where a company has an internal audit function, the audit committee will need to extend its monitoring role to the internal auditors. At least once a year, the committee should meet the internal and external auditors on its own (i.e. without management) so that any issues arising from their work can be freely raised. Between meetings, the committee chairman in particular needs to maintain communication on audit matters both internally and with the external auditors. If there are no internal auditors, the committee should review each year whether there is a need for such a service; if it concludes there is not, it should explain why in the annual report.

☐ The committee has some **specific duties as regards the external auditors**. It recommends the appointment of auditors to the board and approves their fees and the other terms on which they are retained. If there is dissatisfaction with their performance, it may recommend their replacement. In the very unlikely event that the board disagrees with the committee, the arguments on both sides need to be put forward to shareholders in the annual report and AGM papers. Smith also says that the committee should approve the appointment and removal of the head of internal audit.

The committee must keep a close check on the external auditors' independence and objectivity. Is it time for a change, if only to get fresh thinking and a new perspective on some old issues? Are the auditors getting too close to management?

Closely related to the second question is the issue of non-audit services. The independence of the auditors may reasonably be expected to be compromised if they also act as the company's consultants and advisers. Under the US Sarbanes-Oxley legislation (see the box on the following pages), non-audit services such as consultancy and advisory work are severely limited. In the UK, it is left to the audit committee to decide what other services the auditors can provide. The committee needs to develop a specific policy on the matter – it may, for example, rule against some services as raising too many potential conflicts (for example, advice on remuneration policy), permit others (such as tax advice) and require a case by case decision on everything else. It may also require non-audit work above a certain financial limit to be approved by the committee.

Where non-audit services are performed, disclosures are required in the annual report, and the committee must explain how auditor objectivity and independence are to be preserved. The need to maintain independence and objectivity also means that the audit committee should develop a policy regulating the employment of former employees of the auditors.

THE SARBANES-OXLEY ACT

A detailed examination of the US Sarbanes-Oxley Act of 2002 (SOX), passed in the aftermath of the Enron, Tyco and other corporate scandals, is outside the scope of this book. But no examination of corporate governance would be complete without reference to SOX and an acknowledgment that there are a few circumstances where it may affect UK companies and their directors.

SOX applies to all companies, whether incorporated in the US or elsewhere, that publicly issue securities in the US and file reports with the US Securities and Exchange Commission (SEC). It has no direct application to other companies. US and non-US subsidiaries outside the terms of the Act may, however, be indirectly affected if their parents have to comply.

Examples of UK companies that are directly affected include Cadbury Schweppes and British Airways, which have securities traded on the New York Stock Exchange.

SOX has a broad application, and much of the detail has been left to the SEC to work through. Among other things, the Act requires the chief executive officer and chief financial officer of a company to certify the annual and quarterly reports under separate civil and criminal provisions. Both must confirm that they have reviewed the reports and that there are no material mis-statements. Individuals who knowingly sign false certificates can face fines and severe criminal penalties. They can also end up forfeiting cash bonuses and share awards.

In addition, SEC rules require management to include a report on their internal controls and procedures for financial reporting in their annual reports filed with the SEC. Management must evaluate the effectiveness of those controls and procedures, and

- ☐ The audit committee has a role in fraud prevention. It needs to be confident that there are opportunities throughout the company for employees to act as "whistleblowers" and report improprieties and abuses. This may mean giving employees contact details for committee members for use if other avenues fail. Many companies have introduced confidential fraud hotlines for employees; others use an outside agency that can take calls and forward the information given to the right person. A fraud response plan will be needed to guide investigations into any allegations of wrongdoing.

The Companies Act 2006 has for the first time allowed accountancy firms to limit their liability on company audits but, as we have seen in the opening chapter, the limitation must first be agreed with the company and subsequently by the company's shareholders. No doubt negotiation of the limitation, and presentation of that agreement to shareholders for approval, will be a new task for the audit committee.

the company's auditors must issue a report on the assessment.

These requirements are likely to have a knock-on effect on directors and managers in UK subsidiary companies, who may be asked to provide similar certificates and confirmations in respect of their own financial reporting and internal controls. Such reports will give reassurance and perhaps some legal protection to US officers and management; at the very least, they will demonstrate that the US officers have asked the right questions and received replies that it is reasonable for them to rely on.

Because directors and managers of a UK subsidiary are not directly subject to the SOX provisions nothing they do or fail to do should constitute a breach of the Act or the SEC rules. Even if it did, the US authorities would have no jurisdiction to bring a prosecution in the UK (although the threat of extradition cannot be ignored).

Of course, giving a negligent, reckless or fraudulent certificate or report to the parent company may be regarded as a disciplinary offence and, in the worst cases, mean summary dismissal. It is also conceivable that the parent company and/or a US director or manager who relied on a certificate or report from a UK director or manager may attempt to claim against them if some liability in the US had resulted. The threat of such a claim cannot be discounted; any reports and certificates requested from the US should be prepared and verified with the highest standards of care.

The risks can be minimised if internal controls and procedures in a UK subsidiary mirror those in the US parent. Budgets and resources should be made available for such controls and procedures and, where necessary, for external advice and reports.

Resources and rewards for committee members

The audit committee needs to be adequately resourced. It should have access to outside advice when necessary. And the Smith guidance accepts that committee members should be paid further remuneration in addition to other fees to reflect the onerous nature of their duties and responsibilities. The chairman should command a higher level of remuneration than his colleagues.

Relations between the committee and management

The effectiveness of the committee is obviously closely linked to the effectiveness of senior managers. Management should not wait for the audit committee to ask for information. It needs to ensure that the audit committee is kept informed at all times and to take the initiative in supplying information to it.

16. Internal control

"The board should maintain a sound system of internal control to safeguard shareholders' investment and the company's assets" – *main principle C.2.*

The Code recommends that the board (or the audit or risk committee) annually reviews the system of internal controls and reports to shareholders that it has done so. The review, it says, should cover "all material controls, including financial, operational and compliance controls and risk management systems".

The Turnbull Guidance suggests ways of applying this part of the Code. It acknowledges that risk-taking entrepreneurship is an essential part of any business and that the purpose of internal controls is to manage risk rather than to try to eliminate it. (In other words, it says that no system can guard against every adverse event, but that a sound one can improve the chances of identifying another Nick Leeson or of spotting the kinds of weaknesses that led Shell to mis-state its oil reserves.)

The system of internal control needs to be an integral part of normal business processes. It needs to operate throughout the year: it should not just be a box-ticking exercise done every 12 months to keep the compliance officer happy. Since risks change as the company's business and the commercial environment in which it operates change, they must be reviewed and assessed regularly.

The Turnbull Guidance says that:

- ☐ the board must set the company's policies for internal control; it is then up to management to implement those policies;

- ☐ the policies must enable the company to respond to the risks it faces and so safeguard its assets against loss and fraud, and identify and manage the liabilities it faces;

- ☐ the board (or an audit or risk committee) needs regularly to ask the right questions and to get the right answers to satisfy itself that the risks facing the company are being managed properly. This requires a good system of regular reporting throughout the company – so that important information from employees reaches the board.

The annual report needs to describe the system of internal control and explain any failure to comply with the Turnbull Guidance.

17. Relations with shareholders

Despite some impressions to the contrary, the Code makes it clear that good governance is not a one-way street. Companies and their boards have numerous obligations and duties to shareholders, but there are reciprocal duties owed by the shareholders to the company.

In the interests of good governance, investors should:

☐ communicate with directors;

☐ "police" boardroom practices – i.e. monitor compliance with the Code.

Communication

Main principle D.1 says that there should be a dialogue between the board and shareholders **"based on the mutual understanding of objectives"**. Main principle E.1 says: **"Institutional shareholders should enter into a dialogue with companies based on the mutual understanding of objectives"**. Yes, the board has to explain to shareholders what it is about, where it wants to get to and how it is going to meet its aims; but equally shareholders must make sure they clearly state their objectives and the timescale in which they want them achieved.

In talking about dialogue with shareholders, the Code refers largely to major investors. There are two reasons for this:

☐ the Code originated as a response to pressure from large institutional shareholders for reform of boardroom practice;

☐ practicalities dictate that no board is going to spend time or money talking to every shareholder with a few hundred shares; the priority will be investors with a large proportion of the share capital – and in most listed companies these will be pension funds, insurance companies and other investment managers.

While this focus on big investors, is natural, perhaps even inevitable, it highlights a potential flaw in the Code. It could be seen as marginalising or ignoring those investors who, though small, still have rights. In many places, the Code openly refers to consultations with "major shareholders", and main principle D.1 is headed "Dialogue with Institutional Shareholders". An inconspicuous footnote maintains the legalities by stating: "Nothing in these principles or provisions should be taken to override the general requirements of law to treat shareholders equally in access to information."

THE BUSINESS REVIEW

All companies, public and private, need to produce a Business Review as part of their Directors' Report. (This replaces the unlamented Operating and Financial Review abolished by Gordon Brown in a fit of de-regulatory enthusiasm.) The only exception is for "small companies", which are defined as private companies that can satisfy any two of three conditions on turnover (not more than £5.6m), balance sheet total (not more than £2.8m) and employees (not more than 50). The Companies Act 2006 gives the Review a new focus: it is to inform shareholders and help them to assess how the directors have performed their duty to promote the success of the company (see chapter 2).

To that end, the Business Review must contain:

- a fair review of the company's business;
- a description of the principal risks and uncertainties facing the company;
- a balanced and comprehensive analysis of the development and performance of the business during the year, and its position at the end of the year;
- to the extent necessary to understand the business, an analysis using financial key performance indicators and other KPIs, particularly those on environmental and employee matters.

A UK listed company (not one whose shares are traded on AIM or PLUS) needs additional disclosures in its Business Review (to the extent they are necessary for an understanding of the business):

- the main trends and factors likely to affect future development and performance;
- information about the impact of the business on the environment, plus information on employees and "social and community issues";
- information about people with whom the company has contractual or other arrangements that are "essential" to the business.

That last point was a late amendment to the Companies Act 2006 and at the time came in for criticism from the business world. The government emphasised that it was designed to lead to disclosure of key relationships, such as reliance on a sole supplier or customer where the loss of a contract would have a serious knock-on effect. But contracts are not the only target: the government minister made it clear that key employees and even regulators may be essential to a business and could lead to disclosures.

One welcome relief is that no impending development or negotiation needs to be disclosed if that disclosure would be seriously prejudicial to the company. Nor is the Review subject to an audit; although directors will commit a criminal offence if they fail to comply with these requirements.

It is a difficult balancing act to maintain, keeping your major shareholders informed of the latest developments and consulting them on major issues of interest to them without putting them in a privileged position. Confidential briefings for analysts and major shareholders were criticised as being exclusive and unfair to small investors, and are now closely regulated; in recent years it has become common for them to be done by webcasts that any shareholder can log into, with copies of presentations by the chief executive being available on a company's website.

The reality is that major shareholders will usually make their views known to the board by talking to the chief executive, the chairman or the senior independent director at what may be a regular meeting: the Code encourages non-executive directors to "develop an understanding of the views of major shareholders" through face-to-face contact, briefings with brokers and analysts and surveys of shareholder opinion. Smaller shareholders have the forum of the annual general meeting where, if they are sufficiently vocal, their protests may hit the mass media and so apply pressure to the board in that way.

Compliance

In assessing a company's compliance with the corporate governance regime set out in the Code, institutional shareholders are urged to "give due weight to all relevant factors drawn to their attention". They need to factor into their assessment "the size and complexity of the company and the nature of the risks and challenges it faces". In other words, they need to understand the issues and considerations that will have influenced the board. Shareholders should not adopt a box-ticking approach and ignore the explanations proffered by a board for non-compliance. Rather, they should give the company their reasoned views if they disagree and be prepared to enter into a dialogue with the board if differences remain.

In trying to police the board and exert pressure for reform, institutional shareholders need to ensure that they use the considerable voting power they have. There have been a number of cases where particularly vocal shareholders have failed to vote as a result, it would seem, of difficulties in passing instructions down the line to the nominees or agents who complete the proxy forms or attend the meetings on their behalf. As we have seen, one objective of the company law reform process, which resulted in the Companies Act 2006, was to "enhance shareholder engagement", and to that end the government has taken (but not yet used) the power to compel institutional shareholders to disclose their voting records.

18. Corporate social responsibility

Although no part of the Code is specifically concerned with corporate social responsibility (CSR), there is some recognition that a company's duties extend beyond its shareholders.

"The board should set the company's values and standards and ensure that its obligations to its shareholders and others are understood and met" – *supporting principles, A.1.*

Moreover, the Turnbull Guidance makes clear that risk assessment should cover not only narrow financial risks but also those related to "health, safety and environmental, reputation, and business probity issues".

The Companies Act 2006 has now added to those pressures by requiring directors to have regard to community and environmental issues when considering their duty to promote the success of their company (see chapter 2) and by the disclosures to be included in the Business Review (see box, page 68).

Increasingly, CSR is seen as part of best practice by both the City and the government. The Association of British Insurers, whose members own more than 20 per cent of the companies on the London Stock Exchange, publishes guidance on CSR-related issues for both companies and investors. Its 2007 "Socially Responsible Investment Guidelines" ask that the annual report highlights a company's environmental, social and governance (ESG) risks. A remuneration committee should also disclose whether it considers corporate performance on ESG issues when setting remuneration for senior executives, and whether an incentive structure may inadvertently encourage "irresponsible" ESG behaviour.

The government sponsors a CSR website, on which it says it has "an ambitious vision for UK businesses to consider the economic, social and environmental impacts of their activities, wherever they operate in the world".

Big companies such as BP and Unilever are keen to talk about social and environmental issues in their annual reports, and many people argue that complying with CSR guidelines attracts customers, differentiates you from the competition and can have a positive effect on the share price. The growing number of "green" and ethical investment funds needs to find "green" and ethical businesses to invest in.

The charity Business in the Community claims a membership of over 700 of the UK's top companies "committed to improving their positive impact on society". It publishes a Corporate Responsibility Index, which measures the performance of companies in terms of how well they apply CSR values to their business.

For bigger companies in particular, CSR is, it can be argued, not an add-on or an optional extra: it is an integral part of good governance.

FURTHER INFORMATION; USEFUL WEBSITES

The Combined Code on Corporate Governance, June 2006
www.frc.org.uk/corporate

The Governance Code of Practice for Universities
www.sheffield.ac.uk/cuc

Guidance from the Independent Commission on Good Governance in Public Services
www.opm.co.uk/ICGGPS/index.htm

The Myners review on the governance of mutual life companies
www.hm-treasury.gov.uk

The Institute of Directors publishes *Standards for the Board* and offers a wide range of information, advice and training for directors and boards
www.iod.com

The Institute of Chartered Secretaries and Administrators publishes: guidance on matters reserved for the board; a sample non-executive appointment letter; guidance on the induction process for new directors; sample terms of reference for board committees.
www.icsa.org.uk/news/guidance.php

Information on corporate social responsibility appears on the government site
www.csr.gov.uk

The Quoted Companies Alliance represents the interests of smaller quoted companies (including those on AIM and PLUS)
www.quotedcompaniesalliance.co.uk

service contracts

CHAPTER 4

1. Introduction

Directors' remuneration has long been a political issue, with media stories of "fat cats" and, more recently, "rewards for failure" fuelling the debate.

The most notable legislative response has been the **2002 Directors' Remuneration Report Regulations ("the Regulations")**, which require preparation of a directors' remuneration report and far greater disclosure of directors' remuneration packages from listed companies. Significantly, the regulations entitle shareholders to an advisory vote on the directors' remuneration report.

In 2003, "no votes" at the annual general meetings of GlaxoSmithKline (GSK) and WPP, and a string of other controversies over executive pay and contracts, led the government to publish a consultation document, "Rewards for Failure – Directors' Remuneration, Contracts, Performance and Severance".

Essentially, the document set out two options: revising practice guidelines; more legislative change. Recent indications are of a move away from the latter. On January 25, 2005, Patricia Hewitt, the then trade and industry secretary, announced that the government had decided against new provisions on directors' remuneration in the Company Law Reform Bill, saying that research by Deloitte, commissioned by the DTI, had shown that the Regulations were having a "positive impact" on pay and severance policies.

Companies, though, are by no means off the hook. Further legislation at some time in the future cannot be ruled out. And new guidelines are inevitable: Hewitt called on the Association of British Insurers (ABI), the National Association of Pension Funds (NAPF) and the Confederation of British Industry (CBI) to develop a common set of best practice guidelines on directors' contracts.

The service contract between a director and an employing company, therefore, is more than a legal agreement and an incentive tool. It is a window on corporate governance.

The practical aspects and make-up of a director's remuneration package are covered in chapter 6. In this chapter, we look at the main aspects of the legal and regulatory framework and consider the major issues for employing companies and individual directors when agreeing service contracts and, crucially, when negotiating termination packages.

2. The general legal and regulatory framework

Directors and employers obviously do not have a clean slate when negotiating a contract. There are several legislative, regulatory and other provisions that determine what is lawful and/or prudent, particularly in the case of a listed company. The following factors should be borne in mind:

☐ directors have, as chapter 2 makes clear, a duty to promote the success of the company at all times. When negotiating and agreeing service contracts, they need to ensure that their conduct is consistent with this duty;

☐ the **Companies Act** (revised in 2006) imposes certain constraints on the length of notice periods/fixed terms;

☐ the **Combined Code on Corporate Governance**, which applies to all listed companies subject to the Listing Rules, imposes requirements regarding the source of instructions (see 3, below), the length of notice periods/fixed terms, the make-up of the remuneration package and the negotiation of termination packages;

☐ the **Institutional Investors' Corporate Governance Statements** set out details of the approach institutional investors expect companies to take in relation to the length of notice periods/fixed terms, the make-up of the remuneration package and severance packages.

So listed companies are increasingly expected to comply with requirements over and above those laid down by statute – i.e. with the recommendations of the Combined Code – and to respect the views of institutional investors. Thus, notice periods shorter than the statutory minimum are becoming common. (The Listing Rules require companies either to comply with the detailed provisions of the Combined Code or explain, in the annual report, why they have not done so; see chapter 3.)

3. General principles of negotiation; source of instructions

There are two key legal and regulatory points:

A director should not be personally involved in their own service agreement and remuneration package.

This means that they should not be responsible for preparing or instructing the company's lawyers in relation to their own contract and should not be involved in the company's decision making about their own service agreement/remuneration.

There should be clarity regarding who has responsibility for negotiating service agreements and remuneration packages for directors.

The Combined Code recommends:

☐   a formal and transparent procedure for developing policy on executive remuneration and for fixing the remuneration packages of individual directors – no director should be involved in deciding their own remuneration;

☐   the board should establish a remuneration committee of at least three, or, in the case of smaller companies, two members. The company chairman may be a member (if previously classed as "independent"); the other members should all be independent non-executive directors (see chapter 3, section 14);

☐   remuneration committees should have delegated responsibility for setting remuneration for all executive directors and the chairman, and this should extend to pension rights and any compensation payments.

4.   Length of fixed terms/notice periods

Specifics of law and regulation

The **Companies Act 2006** says that:

☐   contracts of more than two years' duration need to be approved by shareholders in general meeting. In the absence of such an approval, the term is void and the contract terminable on reasonable notice. (The equivalent provision under the Companies Act 1985 applied to contracts of more than five years' duration);

☐   a director's contract must be available for inspection by shareholders – under the Companies Act 1985, this applied only where the contract was for a fixed term of 12 months or more or was terminable on notice of 12 months or more.

Under the **code of directors' duties:**

☐   where a contract provides for a particularly long term there is the risk of a challenge by shareholders on the grounds that, in agreeing to the provision, the directors failed to put the company's interests first and consequently were in breach of the code of directors' duties. (It is therefore advisable for any board/remuneration committee employing directors on long-term contracts to minute the reasons why.)

Under the **Listing Rules**:

☐ a listed company's report to shareholders on directors' remuneration must include details of any directors' service contracts with a notice period in excess of one year or with provisions for pre-determined compensation on termination exceeding one year's salary and benefits, giving the reasons for such a notice period/pre-determined compensation;

☐ all directors' contracts have to be available for shareholder inspection.

The Combined Code says that:

☐ notice or contract periods should be set at one year or less;

☐ if it is necessary to offer longer notice or contract periods to new directors recruited from outside, such periods should reduce to one year or less after the initial period.

(Two-year rolling contracts have come under fire from shareholders – for example, at the AGMs of GSK and Tesco in 2003.)

Negotiation points

From the employing company's perspective

Notice periods/fixed terms that exceed 12, perhaps even six, months may not be in the company's best interests – irrespective of the seniority and importance of the director. There are several reasons why:

☐ they are impractical: few companies want directors who have decided to leave continuing to work for them for a long period. They will usually agree to allow the director to go before their notice expires – or put them on "garden leave" (but enforcing garden leave for more than six months can be difficult; see 7, below);

☐ they have cost implications: the longer the notice period, the larger the potential pay off if the company chooses to terminate the employment;

☐ they can antagonise investors: institutional and other shareholders prefer shorter notice periods and fixed terms so as to limit the company's exposure on termination.

The argument that lengthier periods are necessary to attract high-calibre people seldom holds water. Top performing individuals do not need the security of long contracts: they can reasonably be expected to find another position within six months and so mitigate their losses. If there are exceptional circumstances that justify a longer term it may, as the Combined Code advises, be best to reflect this through an initial term followed by a shorter notice period.

Long notice periods and fixed terms look increasingly anachronistic. The Deloitte report for the DTI on the impact of the Regulations concluded that there has been "a rapid and almost complete reduction in directors' notice periods to one year or less". The report included data showing that while 32 per cent of FTSE 100 directors had notice periods of two years in 2001, this had fallen to just one per cent by 2004.

From the director's perspective

For a director, a lengthy notice period can be a double-edged sword. On the one hand, it provides financial security should things go wrong. On the other, it acts as a straitjacket: combined with a well-drafted garden leave provision, the notice period gives the company a hold on the director and can be used to limit their ability to move to an attractive position with another company.

Much will depend on personal circumstances. Where a director has concerns about their ability to secure another position quickly, perhaps because of their age or the economic climate, then it is in their interests to negotiate as lengthy a notice period as possible. Where a director is very confident about their position in the marketplace, and possibly sees their current job as a stepping stone to greater things elsewhere, a shorter notice period may be desirable.

In negotiations, the following are likely to be relevant:

☐ **current notice:** someone who has previously enjoyed the security of a six months' notice period may reasonably expect the same from a new employer;

☐ **risk:** if the director is being recruited into a new sector they may seek to argue for a longer notice period on the basis that it will be more difficult for them to secure another position swiftly. They may also want added security if the company has a reputation for hiring and firing directors, is in a particularly volatile marketplace or is otherwise unstable;

☐ **reward:** sometimes the director is lured by the promise of "jam tomorrow". Where, for example, the company has plans to float on the Stock Exchange, the director will want to know they will be employed long enough to reap financial benefits.

From both perspectives

It is important that both the company and the individual director understand exactly what has been agreed in relation to the contract term. They should, therefore:

☐ avoid jargon when negotiating/instructing lawyers; the meaning of terms such as "rolling" or "evergreen" contracts is often disputed between employment lawyers;

☐ be very precise about how the notice period/fixed term should work;

☐ make any provision as simple to understand and operate as possible;

☐ avoid complex arrangements whereby notice can only be served on particular dates/during particular periods etc.

5. Payment in lieu clauses

Purpose

A payment in lieu clause allows an employer to terminate someone's employment instantly on making a payment in lieu of salary or salary and benefits during a notice period or, possibly, a portion of the salary otherwise due.

It means more flexibility for the employer, entitling a company to bring an employment relationship to an end and quickly introduce a replacement.

Without it, companies that dismiss with no notice are in breach of contract and therefore at risk of legal action – i.e. a claim for wrongful dismissal.

Payment in lieu provisions are particularly important where:

☐ the contract has restrictive covenants (see 7, below) – these cannot be relied upon in cases of wrongful dismissal;

☐ the director holds equity in the company and the amount they are entitled to be paid for a return of their shares depends on whether they have been wrongfully dismissed/how long they have been employed before termination.

Tax implications

Where a payment is made by a company under a payment in lieu provision it is regarded by the Inland Revenue as an emolument deriving from the employee's employment contract. This means that the £30,000 tax exemption for a severance payment will not be available: the full amount of the severance payment (or at least that portion representing the payment in lieu) will be liable for tax and national insurance.

Negotiation points

Payment in lieu provisions need very careful drafting and will frequently be the subject of negotiation. Advice should be sought from an employment lawyer, but companies should bear in mind the points below.

- [ ] It should be absolutely clear that payment in lieu will be at the discretion/election of the company. Otherwise, a director will be able to argue that they are automatically entitled to a payment in lieu where the company chooses to terminate. The courts have made clear that, where an entitlement under a payment in lieu provision has arisen, an employee can receive the appropriate sum as a debt without deduction for mitigation or accelerated receipt. This means it is in the company's best interests for payment in lieu to be optional; in some circumstances, it may be preferable to dismiss instantly and then negotiate a package taking proper account of mitigation.

- [ ] Care should be taken when deciding the amount of the payment/the formula to calculate it. The company may wish to negotiate/be seen to negotiate a payment in lieu provision that does take some account of mitigation – i.e. an executive's likely losses on termination. This is often achieved by including a formula where a payment in lieu only reflects salary, not salary and benefits. If a director is to be employed on a lengthy notice period, a company may well wish, however, to include further provision for mitigation. Another option is to draft the provision so that the company can elect to make the payment in lieu in instalments, the right to such payment terminating on the director starting in a new position.

6.　The remuneration package

Legal and regulatory background

Directors' service contracts must be drawn up with regard to both legal and regulatory provisions on pay. This means being aware not only of restrictions on directors' involvement in decisions about their own contracts (see 3, above), but also of best-practice guidelines for listed companies on pay levels and the make-up of the pay package. The Combined Code states that:

"Levels of remuneration should be sufficient to attract, retain and motivate directors of the quality required to run the company successfully, but a company should avoid paying more than is necessary for this purpose. A significant proportion of executive directors' remuneration should be structured so as to link rewards to corporate and individual performance."

Basic salary

The company should bear in mind that:

☐ articles of association will often limit the amount the company can pay in **directors' fees.** The service contract should therefore make clear that salary payable is inclusive of any fees or other remuneration to which the director may be entitled from the company or any group company. This will avoid argument over how much remuneration is referable to fees and enable the company to comply with any limits;

☐ provisions regarding salary reviews – when they will take place, how they will be carried out – should be set out clearly to avoid future dispute. If a contractual right to an increase is not intended there should be wording making this clear;

☐ the practice of increasing directors' pay shortly before retirement and thereby significantly increasing their entitlement under a company's final salary scheme carries risks. It could be deemed to be against the company's best interests. The Combined Code provides that:

"The remuneration committee should consider the pension consequences and associated costs to the company of basic salary increases and other changes in pensionable remuneration, especially for directors close to retirement."

Bonus

To avoid future dispute, both the employing company and an individual director need to ensure that bonus provisions are clear and fully understood. The key points to remember are listed below.

☐ The first major issue to determine is whether the director will have a clear cut contractual entitlement to a bonus according to a particular formula or merely a right to be considered for a bonus by the board/remuneration committee. If the intent is the latter, very careful drafting will be needed.

☐ An employing company also needs to be aware that, even where a bonus scheme is discretionary, there will be constraints on the decisions that can be made. This follows the High Court case *Clark v Nomura* in which it was held that "even a simple discretion whether to award a bonus must not be exercised capriciously" and an employer should not exercise its discretion in an "irrational or perverse way" – i.e. a way in which "no reasonable employer would have exercised its discretion".

This does not make it straightforward for an employee to challenge bonus decisions, however. In the 2006 case of *Commerzbank AG v Keene*, in which a very high paid investment banker sought to challenge the level of his bonus, the Court of Appeal indicated that:

"It would require an overwhelming case to persuade the court to find that the level of a discretionary bonus payment was irrational or perverse in an area where so much must depend on the discretionary judgment of the bank in fluctuating market and labour conditions."

While this decision concerns discretionary bonuses in the investment banking sector, it is significant in relation to discretionary bonuses generally. The ruling does make clear that the courts are generally reluctant to review an employer's decision regarding the level of a discretionary bonus.

☐ Decisions regarding the level of discretionary bonus payments are prone to allegations of discrimination. A particularly high profile instance of this was the case of *Bower v Schroder Securities Limited* in which another senior investment banker was awarded £1.4m in compensation for (what she claimed was) an "insultingly low" award. (She received a bonus of £25,000 when comparable male colleagues were awarded bonuses of £440,000 and £650,000.)

☐ Board/remuneration committees should also take into account Combined Code guidance, which underlines the link between pay and performance:

"The remuneration committee should consider whether the directors should be eligible for annual bonuses. If so, performance conditions should be relevant, stretching and designed to enhance the business. Upper limits should be set and disclosed. There may be a case for part payment in shares to be held for a significant period."

☐ If a service contract is to contain detailed provision about the calculation of the bonus, it will often be desirable to put this within a separate schedule. Such a schedule may specify:

when the bonus is payable;

whether the bonus is to be payable during part years when the director's employment has begun/ended and, if so, how any pro rata bonus payment is to be calculated;

who is to decide the final figure;

whether the bonus will always be payable on termination or only in certain circumstances;

how particular terms such as "net profits" etc. are to be defined;

whether bonus forms part of pensionable earnings. (The Combined Code recommends that it should not);

whether there will be express performance criteria. (As stated above, the Combined Code recommends that there should be performance conditions and that they should be designed to enhance shareholder value);

whether there will, in accordance with Combined Code guidelines, be provision for a limit on the amount of bonus payable.

☐ It may be sensible to have any detailed provision regarding bonus, including calculations derived from net profits, reviewed and approved by the company's auditors, particularly if the service contract will provide for reference to the auditors in the event of dispute.

Pensions

The service agreement must clearly provide for:

☐ the director's entitlement to pension, subject to the rules of the scheme;

☐ the employing company's entitlement to withdraw or amend the rules or benefits of a particular pension scheme and/or to terminate an individual's participation within it at any time. (Obviously, the director is likely to want assurance that, in the event of this type of provision being relied on, equivalent replacement benefits will be provided.)

It is also now of crucial importance that companies review provisions to reflect the significant changes in tax treatment of pension contributions, effective from April 2006. (See chapter 5.)

Permanent health insurance

Permanent health insurance (PHI) is designed to secure income for employees unable to work through sickness or injury. A PHI policy will usually be taken out by a company for a number of senior employees. The insurance provider will pay sums to the company after the employee has been ill for a specified period; payments will be made until the employee is able to return to work. A typical provision within a director's service contract may, therefore, entitle a director to six months' contractual sick pay and, thereafter, sums from the company as received under its PHI scheme.

While this is all very well in theory, in practice PHI can be a troublesome benefit. There is often a gulf between employees' perception of the scheme and the reality of it how it operates.

A PHI policy will usually only provide cover for someone while they remain employed by the company. When an employee is dismissed because of long-term absence through illness (or for any other reason), their entitlement to PHI benefits automatically ceases. The understanding of employees, however, is often that PHI protects them against the impact of long-term illness and that they will continue to receive benefits for as long as they are ill – whether or not the employer chooses to dismiss them.

PHI entitlements have been the subject of a number of disputes. The leading case is that of *Aspden v. Webbs Poultry and Meat Group*, in which it was held that an employee's contract contained an implied term that their employer would not dismiss them while sick if dismissal would lead to loss of entitlement to benefits under a PHI scheme.

The Aspden decision means that PHI provisions need very careful drafting and demand expert help. A common solution is for the contract to provide that:

- ☐ the employing company will not terminate where an individual is absent through illness and is, or may become, entitled to PHI benefits;

- ☐ the employing company will still be entitled to dismiss in certain specified circumstances – for example, gross misconduct, redundancy or where the individual ceases to be eligible for benefits under the PHI scheme.

Employers must make it expressly clear that an employee's entitlement to PHI is subject to the rules of the particular scheme. Failure to do so can be an expensive mistake: where the contractual promise exceeds the real levels of cover under the scheme the employer can find itself obliged to give benefits it will not be able to recover.

Share options

Provision for share options should not be made in a service agreement but rather in a separate side letter/agreement. This will ensure that:

☐ the director's entitlement to share options depends entirely upon the provisions of the share option scheme;

☐ the director will not be entitled to seek compensation for loss of share options as part of a wrongful dismissal claim.

7. Restrictive covenants

Purpose

The directors, as the most senior employees of a company, are likely to have strong relationships with the company's key customers, intimate knowledge of the company's most confidential information and, quite possibly, significant sway over the company's employees, many of whom they will probably have recruited. Given this, it is prudent for a company to protect itself against the risk of future competitive activity from a departing director. The mechanism for doing so is restrictive covenants.

There is an anecdotal view in some sectors that covenants are "not worth the paper they are written on". While it is true that justifying the need and scope of covenants can be difficult, costing the company significant amounts in management time and legal fees, the UK courts do have a track record of enforcing appropriate and properly drafted restrictions.

Starting position of UK courts (restraint of trade doctrine)

A UK court will only enforce a particular covenant if:

☐ it is satisfied, on reviewing the evidence, that the covenant is necessary to protect the company's legitimate business interests (historically, client connections, confidential information and workforce stability);

☐ the particular covenant is drafted so as to provide the minimum necessary protection to those interests.

This reflects the need to protect and uphold the principle of free trade.

Ensuring enforceability

The key to enforceability is making sure that any covenant can be seen to have been tailored to the particular business of the company and the role that the employee will be carrying out. A long non-solicitation of customers covenant may be appropriate where a company has a limited number of important clients with whom it has developed a close relationship over time and from whom it receives instructions on a fairly infrequent basis – for example, once a year; it will be less easy to justify where a company has a significant number of more "arm's length" customers who buy its products/services very frequently. Similarly, a 12-month non-solicitation restriction may be right for a sales director who has very close relationships with key customers and in-depth knowledge of their requirements but "wrong" for a junior employee or a finance director who has no direct dealings with customers.

As a rule of thumb, courts will be reluctant to enforce employment covenants for more than a 12-month period. Six-month covenants will be easier to enforce, particularly in the case of non-compete restrictions (see below).

In cases where the departure of a director could be a real competitive threat to the business, detailed instructions should be given to a specialist employment lawyer so that covenants can be properly tailored and drafted.

Types of covenant

Non-compete covenants

These have often been viewed as unreasonable, extreme and, therefore, as difficult to enforce. A court will ask why sufficient protection to the business could not be provided by less stringent clauses (e.g. non-solicitation, non-dealing and non-poaching covenants or an express confidentiality provision) and will question the company's right to preclude an individual from joining a competitor.

It may, however, be possible to justify a non-compete provision where:

- [ ] the company has a very local clientele that may be expected to follow a departing employee; thus, a hairdresser or estate agent may be justified in preventing someone from leaving and setting up in opposition in the same street;

- [ ] the company can prove that significant technical or other business-critical information that is not necessarily client-specific and, therefore, not necessarily safeguarded by non-solicitation/dealing covenants could not be adequately protected through an express confidentiality provision.

A 2007 decision by the Court of Appeal has confirmed that appropriately drafted non-compete restrictions will be enforceable. In the case of *Thomas v Farr plc,* the Court upheld a 12-month non-compete restriction for a managing director on the grounds that the employer had demonstrated that it had a legitimate business interest in protecting commercially sensitive information. Since this information was not client-specific, it could not have been adequately protected by a non-solicitation or dealing covenant or by a pure confidentiality provision. The fact that it would be difficult for both employee and employer to draw the line between information that remained confidential post-termination and information that did not, only strengthened the argument for a non-competition clause.

As stated above, the length of the restriction will be key. So, too, will its geographical scope: if a director has been primarily responsible for and had knowledge of a company's business in the south east, a clause preventing them from competing anywhere in the UK is likely to be held to be too wide and, therefore, unenforceable.

Non-solicitation covenants

The easiest type of covenant to enforce is usually that precluding an ex-director from soliciting his former employer's clients for a period following termination. Provided the length of the period is reasonable, and the covenant only covers the previous employer's line of business and those clients with whom the director has had individual dealings or of whom he has individual knowledge, a well drafted non-solicitation of clients clause should be enforceable.

Non-dealing covenants

A non-dealing covenant not only precludes active solicitation of the former employer's clients but also acceptance of work from the former employer's clients – even when it is they who make the initial contact. Nonetheless, non-dealing restrictions can be enforceable. This is particularly true if the policing of a non-solicitation clause is likely to prove difficult.

Where non-solicitation and non-dealing restrictions are part of the same contract, they should be contained in **severable sub-clauses**. This way, the employer will still be able to call on the non-solicitation clause if the non-dealing restriction is found to be too wide and, therefore, unenforceable.

In sectors where an employer may need to go through a lengthy tendering process for a contract or where the company invests heavily in building up contacts with potential clients, the company may wish to protect those potential leads as well as existing ones. The scope of non-solicitation and non-dealing covenants may thus extend beyond established customers.

Non-poaching covenants

The position on clauses to prevent a departing director recruiting former colleagues was in doubt for some years. Several cases have now made clear that, in the right circumstances, a UK court will enforce a non-poaching restriction.

The keys to enforceability are to ensure that the covenant:

- is drafted only to cover those who may be expected to have particular knowledge of/influence with clients or knowledge of a company's confidential information;

- is of reasonable duration.

Where a company is particularly concerned about the risk of poaching by a departing director it should consider further provisions. It could, for example:

- expressly specify that information about employees' salaries and remuneration is confidential;

- place directors and other senior employees under a contractual obligation to notify the company if a colleague or former colleague seeks to solicit them.

Non-interference with suppliers covenants

These covenants can be useful where a company is very reliant on relationships with certain key suppliers. They should be drafted to preclude interference with those relationships (and to make clear that they do not apply to the suppliers of general utilities).

Covenants and garden leave

Most companies will wish to protect themselves from competitive activity by a departing director not just through restrictive covenants but also through a "garden leave" clause. On "garden leave", an individual remains employed but is not given any duties. They serve out all or some of their notice at home, tending, the popular fiction is, to their garden.

Provided the clause is properly drafted, the individual will remain under a contractual and fiduciary obligation not to compete in any way with the company for the duration of the garden leave. Further restrictions will prohibit contact with customers or clients and deny access to offices etc. The company therefore gets a breathing space – time to shore up customer contacts etc. before the individual's departure.

The relationship between garden leave clauses and restrictive covenants has been a topic of debate. Should a company that wishes to rely on a restrictive covenant give credit for any period of garden leave? The leading case on the issue makes clear that this will not always be necessary. In practice, however, covenants are generally now drafted to apply for a particular period less any period of garden leave served.

Other related clauses

Well-drafted service agreements will contain various other provisions to make restrictive covenants more effective. They should, for example:

☐ allow the company to enforce restrictions on behalf of other group companies;

☐ oblige a director to make any prospective new employer aware of the terms of the restrictive covenants that apply to them. (New employers who ignore the terms can be sued for inducing a breach of contract);

☐ make clear that the director should not have any other business interests during the period of employment;

☐ include an express confidentiality clause. Where particular categories of sensitive information exist, these should ideally be specified within the clause and, also, treated as confidential within the company.

Enforcement

The detail of how restrictive covenants may be enforced through an injunction or action for damages is beyond the scope of this text. The key point for a company that believes that an employee may have acted in breach of a covenant is to act quickly. Injunctions can prevent ex-employees and their new employers from taking certain steps but they are emergency measures; courts will be reluctant to grant them if they feel the company has been late in seeking relief.

8. Change of control/"golden parachute" clauses

Purpose

Change of control provisions entitle directors to enhanced severance packages in the event of companies being taken over or merged. They are known colloquially as "golden parachute clauses". A fairly typical feature of directors' service agreements in the 1980s, they became less common after the Cadbury, Greenbury and Hampel reports led to closer scrutiny of executives' contracts and of provisions for termination payments.

The usual justification for change of control clauses was that they provided security to directors who would not otherwise join or remain. Over time, however, this has lost credibility. The following arguments are likely to be made against change of control provisions:

- [ ] directors' contracts often include long notice periods; these should be security enough. New owners of a company may lawfully terminate a director's employment without notice only if there are grounds for summary dismissal;

- [ ] directors who are demoted after a takeover are protected by law: they can resign, claim constructive dismissal and seek damages consistent with their loss.

Enforceability

Code of directors' duties

To be justified, change of control provisions must be consistent with the code of directors' duties. As stated in chapter 2, the code obliges directors to:

- [ ] promote the success of the company;
- [ ] act within their powers and use them for a proper purpose;
- [ ] avoid putting themselves in a position where their personal interests conflict with their duties as a director.

If the provision for payment seems to be excessive and out of proportion with the benefit to the company, it can be challenged as a breach of these duties. The same applies if there is any evidence to suggest that the provision's primary purpose was to act as a "poisoned pill" to deter a potential takeover bidder.

If the board and the remuneration committee believe that change of control provisions are necessary, it is advisable for them to minute the reasons why. They should be confident they can justify them as being consistent with the company's best interests; disclosure is likely to be necessary within the directors' remuneration report.

City Code on Takeovers and Mergers (the "Code")

Expert advice should be sought by any public company that wishes to consider amending directors' service agreements in light of a possible takeover.

The City Code on Takeovers and Mergers provides that companies that are the targets of bona fide offers, or that expect to be so imminently, must not enter into a contract "otherwise than in the ordinary course of business" unless they have obtained the prior approval of shareholders in general meeting. It also says that:

"The Panel [on Takeovers and Mergers] will regard amending or entering into a service contract with, or creating or varying the terms of employment of, a director as entering into a contract 'otherwise than in the ordinary course of business' ... if the new or amended contract or terms constitute an abnormal increase in the emoluments or a significant improvement in the terms of service. This will not prevent any increase or improvement which results from a genuine promotion or new appointment but the Panel must be consulted in advance in such cases."

The Code applies to all offers for public companies and, thanks to the Companies Act 2006, now has a statutory basis. No public company can ignore its provisions.

Liquidated damages clauses and penalty clauses

Where advance provision is made for the damages payable to one party as a result of a breach of contract by the other, the courts will categorise the position in one of two ways. Liquidated damages clauses are those where the pre-estimate of loss is seen as being genuine; penalty clauses are those where it is not and where the sum stipulated is "extravagant and unconscionable in comparison with the likely level of loss". The former are, in principle, enforceable; the latter are void.

If a change of control clause is to be regarded as advance provision for damages it will be necessary to demonstrate that it was framed on the basis of a genuine pre-estimate of loss. This will require evidence that proper consideration was given to an individual director's likely circumstances on termination and proper account was taken of their duty to mitigate their loss by seeking alternative employment.

There are those who say that change of control clauses should not be regarded as advance provision for damages payable as a result of a breach but as an express contractual provision under which the company/director is entitled to terminate the contract lawfully. While there is case law that supports this argument, the position is by no means certain. If a remuneration committee does decide that a change of control provision may be appropriate, it remains advisable for it to try to ensure that the amount of the proposed payment is a genuine pre-estimate of loss. This is also in a director's individual interests: it helps ensure that the change of control provision can, in due course, be relied upon.

9. Severance

The options

Dismiss summarily for gross misconduct

Where there is clear evidence of dishonesty or other serious misconduct amounting to a repudiatory breach, the company is legally entitled to dismiss the culprit with immediate effect, without any requirement to serve notice or pay in lieu of notice. The need for clear evidence, however, cannot be over-emphasised: in all but the most clear cut of cases, instant dismissal carries a significant risk of litigation; there may be a High Court claim for wrongful dismissal and, possibly, a statutory claim for unfair dismissal as discussed in section 10 below.

Serve notice and require director to work notice period

As stated in section 4, this option may not be in the best interests of the company. Directors who are asked to serve their full notice can be demotivated and even hostile towards the company and the remaining directors. Their main focus will, understandably, be on finding another job rather than ensuring the long-term success of the business. The company will usually prefer to cut ties – and bring in someone else – as soon as possible.

Serve notice and put on garden leave

Garden leave provisions are becoming increasingly common. The main reasons for this have been given in section 7. In summary: garden leave helps limit the threats to a business posed by a director's departure to a rival and can provide more security than covenants. It also gives the company time and space to negotiate a severance package.

The director on garden leave will often approach the company to agree an earlier termination date so that they can take up their new position. Their entitlement to further payment will then cease.

Garden leave is also useful where cashflow makes a lump sum payment in lieu undesirable.

Steps should be taken to ensure the terms of the garden leave are consistent with the director's contractual rights. The director should continue to receive all salary and benefits and should not be financially disadvantaged. An employing company should also ensure that there are very clear instructions about what a director can and cannot do while on garden leave. These should cover: contact with clients, employees or other business contacts; the steps the director is to take if contacted; the extent to which the director can be called upon to carry out particular tasks and provide assistance.

Terminate instantly under express payment in lieu provision

It is also increasingly common for service agreements to allow the company to terminate a director's employment on making a payment in lieu of notice. This provides a mechanism to bring the director's employment to an end instantly without being in breach of contract. Any restrictive covenants will continue to have effect insofar as they are enforceable. Further information about payment in lieu clauses appears in section 5 above.

Initiate a dialogue and negotiate a package

Frequently, the first instinct of the other directors/non-executive directors is to initiate a "cards on the table" chat with a view to negotiating an appropriate package. This can work well, particularly if there is a good relationship between those who will have the discussion, the reasons for the departure are understood and the circumstances are not acrimonious – in other words, if the negotiations are likely to succeed.

Generally, however, there are risks attached. Employment cases make clear that even where there is an agreement to talk off the record "without prejudice", a party may still be able to rely on these discussions to support a legal claim. The risk is particularly acute where there has been no formal prior procedure. In these circumstances, the discussions and the absence of any formalities could be used in an unfair dismissal claim and/or negotiations for a significant sum in addition to contractual severance entitlements.

Legal/regulatory constraints

Sections 215 to 222 of the Companies Act 2006

The above sections (which replace sections 312 to 316 of the Companies Act 1985) preclude payments "of compensation for loss of office" where particulars of the payment have not been approved by a company's shareholders. Generally, though, this will not apply. Section 220(1) of the Act provides for express exclusions in relation to a payment made:

- in good faith;
- in discharge of an existing legal obligation (effectively defined as an obligation that was not entered into in connection with or in consequence of the event giving rise to the payment);
- by way of damages for breach of such an obligation;
- by way of settlement or compromise of any claim arising in connection with the termination of the person's office or employment; or
- by way of pension in respect of past services.

In addition, case law authority says that payments made to a departing director under express contractual provisions – for example, an express payment in lieu or golden parachute clause – are not covered by what was section 312 of the Companies Act 1985. This would certainly still seem to be the case as a result of the express drafting of the new provisions. These sections could be an issue, however, where a proposed payment to a director seems excessive in relation to their legal entitlements.

Code of directors' duties

If there is evidence to suggest that proposed payments are excessive when set against an individual director's legal entitlements, it is possible that the code of directors' duties has been breached and that a challenge from shareholders will follow. Shareholders could argue that directors, in agreeing particular payments for a departing executive, were acting other than in the best interests of the company.

If a payment is proposed that seems out of line with an individual director's contractual entitlement and unfair dismissal rights, the company's remuneration committee or full board ought to minute the reasons why. Such payments will need to be justified.

The Combined Code

The Combined Code says that:

"The remuneration committee should carefully consider what compensation commitments (including pension contributions and all other elements) their directors' terms of appointment would entail in the event of early termination. The aim should be to avoid rewarding poor performance. They should take a robust line on reducing compensation to reflect departing directors' obligations to mitigate loss."

This provision can be useful when negotiating a package on behalf of a listed company. In particular, it can help endorse the point that payments must be closely linked to financial loss. If there is every reason to believe that a director with a 12 months' notice period would find a position within six months following termination, the remuneration committee would probably find a package of more than six months hard to justify to shareholders.

But "avoiding rewarding poor performance" and "taking a proper line to reflect mitigation" are often difficult to reconcile. A director employed under a contract with a 12 months' notice period is, in the absence of gross misconduct, entitled to 12 months' notice irrespective of performance. If they have performed poorly, it may be more difficult for them to find another job and thereby mitigate their loss. In other words, it can be more difficult to negotiate a discount when a director hasn't delivered.

Disclosure requirements

Full disclosure of amounts paid to departing directors is required in the directors' remuneration report, which will then be put to an advisory vote by shareholders. So a board needs to bear in mind the likely reaction of investors before any deal is agreed.

10. Potential legal claims

Wrongful dismissal

A wrongful dismissal is a dismissal that breaches the terms of the contract. If, therefore, a director is entitled to 12 months' notice but is dismissed instantly without notice, the company will be liable for damages; the director will be entitled to a payment equating to the loss of salary and benefits over the 12 months' notice period.

Any damages will, however, be subject to a reduction for mitigation. A dismissed employee is legally required to take reasonable steps to find an alternative job. If they succeed and take up a new position during the notice period, any sum earned will reduce the amount of their loss pound for pound. If a court is not satisfied that an employee has complied with the obligation to mitigate, this will be reflected in its award for compensation.

Successful wrongful dismissal claims prevent the employer from relying on any provisions within the contract: if the employer is held to have breached the contract, it cannot enforce terms such as restrictive covenants, and these will consequently fall away. It is largely because of this that, where restrictive covenants exist, it is now standard practice to add a contractual payment in lieu provision allowing the company to terminate instantly without breaching the contract.

Unfair dismissal

Every person in Great Britain who has been employed for one year or more has a statutory right not to be unfairly dismissed. This right applies just as much to an employed director as any other employee. Dismissal will only be found to be fair if:

- ☐ it is made for a potentially fair reason, such as redundancy, poor performance or poor conduct;

- ☐ before dismissing or serving notice, the employer followed the necessary fair procedure (see below);

- ☐ it is reasonable to dismiss in all the circumstances of the case.

Until quite recently, unfair dismissal was not a significant factor in the majority of cases relating to the termination of directors' contracts. This was because compensation for unfair dismissal was limited when set against a director's contractual entitlement. The potential compensation recoverable for unfair dismissal has now, however, significantly increased. In addition to an entitlement to a basic award (which is still a limited amount calculated in the same way as a statutory redundancy payment), an employee who has been unfairly dismissed is entitled to a compensatory award (dependent on their losses), the statutory maximum for which is now £60,600.

A further significant change took place on October 1, 2004. As a result of new statutory, disciplinary and grievance procedures, an employer must go through a **minimum disciplinary procedure** before dismissing someone. The procedure includes:

- ☐ calling the employee to attend a disciplinary hearing;

☐   providing the employee with details of matters to be discussed before the hearing;

☐   notifying the employee of the decision made after the hearing and providing the right to appeal.

If these minimum procedures are not followed, the dismissal is automatically deemed to be unfair and the compensation awarded can be subject to an uplift of between 10 and 50 per cent.

The appropriateness of unfair dismissal claims will, of course, vary. A director is not entitled to double recovery in relation to the same period of loss. This means, for example, that if a director is being paid in lieu of a 12-month notice period (either under an express clause or as a result of reaching agreement to make a payment in lieu) and they can mitigate their losses within the 12 months by finding another position, legal action will, from a practical point of view, be irrelevant. The director could seek to recover a basic award but this will be little more than a nominal sum. As regards the compensatory award, the director will not be able to demonstrate any losses: they will have been more than compensated by the payment in lieu.

If, on the other hand, a director's actual losses are likely to exceed payments made in relation to their contractual entitlements, an unfair dismissal claim becomes much more relevant. In these circumstances, an employing company that has failed to go through a fair procedure before giving notice could be in trouble. To avoid the risk of litigation, it will be necessary for it to enhance any proposed severance package by a sum in excess of contractual entitlements to reflect potentially recoverable unfair dismissal compensation.

Other

This section has dealt with the most likely actions when a company dismisses a director. It is important to remember, though, that others could arise – for example, the claim that a director's dismissal was on discriminatory grounds.

pensions

CHAPTER 5

This chapter is divided into three parts. The first gives factual information on pension schemes and on the pensions tax regime. The second examines the duties of directors who are trustees of the company pension fund. The third looks at the legal position of directors when the company pension pot falls short.

Part I: The basics

1. Introduction

Pensions often go to the bottom of the pile. They are just too complicated, and there are too many decisions to make. The jargon is off putting and the subject matter is austerely mathematical. But pensions are crucially important: they can be the single biggest expense of a company and one of the most valuable elements of remuneration. You ignore them at your peril.

2. Main types of pension scheme

☐   A defined benefit scheme or final salary scheme promises a certain level of pension once you reach retirement age. It is usually calculated as a proportion of your final salary for each year of service. For example, if you are promised 1/60th of final salary for each year you work for the company and you work for 40 years, you will be paid 40/60ths (i.e. two thirds) of your final salary. On top of that, the law requires an element of inflation-proofing to be built in.

In effect, as long as you keep your side of the bargain and pay in the required level of contributions (typically about five or six per cent of pay), the employer takes all the risk.

There is a downside, though. UK employers that have defined benefit schemes are currently under no obligation to put in enough money to guarantee the pension promise in all circumstances. Employers do have to contribute a certain amount, but this is not nearly enough to pay everyone's pension if the scheme winds up. If the pension scheme winds up, the employer must then fund the benefits in full, but this potentially substantial cost may well be beyond its means. Furthermore, each member does not own a share of the funds; funds will simply be divvied up in accordance with a priority order decided by the government. The Pension Protection

Fund offers an element of protection to members of these schemes that wind up with insufficient funds to provide all the promised benefits. There are restrictions on the level of benefits that are paid from the Pension Protection Fund, so it will not necessarily be as good as getting your benefits from the pension scheme.

- [ ] **A money purchase or defined contribution scheme** makes no promise about what you will get when you retire. You simply contribute to the pension scheme. The money is then invested in the way you have asked. At retirement, you buy a pension with whatever funds are available. The income you get depends on how well the investments have done and how much it costs to buy the pension, as well as other factors such as whether you want any dependant to get a pension on your death and whether you want inflation-proofing built in. So, in money purchase schemes, it is the pension scheme member who takes all the risk. He or she does have a legal right to a share of the funds, but there is no certainty about what that share will be.

  Money purchase schemes can be run by employers or by insurance companies. Those run by insurance companies are known as **personal pension plans** or **stakeholder schemes**. Your employer may contribute, or it may not.

- [ ] **Cash balance schemes** combine elements of the two types of scheme above. They are designed along the lines of a money purchase scheme but the employer promises a certain investment return up to retirement. They are quite popular in the US but have yet to become part of the mainstream in the UK. In essence, both the member and employer share the risk.

3. Unfunded schemes

An unfunded scheme is, as its name implies, not pre-funded. It is little more than a paper promise. The employer promises to pay a certain pension at retirement, but does not put aside any money to do so. This is all very well if your employer is the government, but risky if you work in the private sector. (Unlike the government, private companies can go bust.) A financial promise is only as good as the organisation behind it.

4. Tax breaks

To encourage contributions to schemes, the government offers tax breaks. Anything you pay into a scheme will receive tax relief at your higher marginal income tax rate. Investment returns within the scheme are also tax free. Employers get corporation tax relief on what they contribute.

5. Restrictions

To discourage abuse of the system, there are restrictions on the amount of pension that can be built up each year.

Annual allowance

The annual allowance is the amount of pension you will be allowed to build up each year without incurring tax.

For money purchase schemes, this limit applies to the contributions that you or your employer make. Increases in investments within the scheme are ignored.

For defined benefit schemes, the annual allowance is the annual increase in the capital value of your benefit. The capital value is basically how much more your pension is worth. The government has set down in legislation how this will be calculated.

The annual allowance is £225,000 for 2007/8 and will be increased each year. The government has already announced the annual allowance for the years to 2010/11.

Lifetime allowance

There is a further limit on the amount of pension that can be built up during your life. This lifetime allowance is £1.6m for 2007/8. Again, it will be increased every year; by 2010/11, it will stand at £1.8m.

The amount of pension that you build up in a money purchase scheme is simply the value of your pension account. If you have a final salary benefit, the capital value is the annual pension you are entitled to receive multiplied by 20, plus the value of any additional lump sum benefit.

Pension funds are tested against the lifetime limit each time a new benefit is paid, on death and if you transfer to an overseas scheme. If you take your benefits in stages – for example, if you reduce your working hours and therefore only take part of your pension entitlement – some of your lifetime limit will be used up each time.

Compliance and tax collection

The onus is on **individuals** to ensure that they are within the limits or pay the necessary tax. Pension schemes are also responsible for the payment of the lifetime charge.

The **annual allowance tax** is calculated through the self assessment system. Tax will be charged at 40 per cent on any contributions above the annual allowance.

The **lifetime allowance tax** charge is only payable on pension benefits above the lifetime limit. If you decide to take the excess as a lump sum there will be a one-off tax charge of 55 per cent. If you opt for an additional pension, you will incur a tax charge of 25 per cent on the excess capital value. On top of this, you will be liable for income tax on the additional pension.

Protection of benefits accrued before 2006

The current rules date from April 6, 2006, so-called "A day", when a new pensions regime came into force. The government allows people who were then already close to or above the lifetime limit – £1.5m for 2006/7 – to protect their "retrospective" pension investments. There are two forms of protection available.

☐ **Enhanced protection** allows you to protect benefits accrued before April 6, 2006 from the tax charge provided you comply with the relevant requirements. It means, however, that you can only build up further benefits in limited ways. And if the earnings cap (part of the old regime) applied to you, it will be taken into account when calculating your final pension. Subject to some exceptions, the earnings cap will have applied to you if you joined your pension scheme after 1989. You are able to opt out of enhanced protection if you find that you would be better off without it at any time before you reach 75.

☐ **Primary protection** is only available if the value of your benefits was above the lifetime limit at April 6, 2006.

If you choose this form of protection, your lifetime limit will be increased to the value of your pension benefits at April 6, 2006. This personal lifetime limit will then rise annually by the same percentage as the statutory lifetime allowance. Any growth above this will be taxed. If you choose this form of protection, you will be able to continue to contribute to a pension arrangement, but you will be taxed when you come to take your pension.

To take advantage of one or both of these forms of protection, you will need to register with H M Revenue and Customs by April 5, 2009. If you think that you may need protection, seek independent financial advice as soon as possible.

The investment regime

Investment rules include:

☐ a limit on scheme borrowing to 50 per cent of scheme assets at the date of loan;

☐ a five per cent restriction on shares of the sponsoring employer. Schemes are permitted to invest in residential property, subject to trustee approval.

Phased retirement

Since April 6, 2006, you've been able to continue working and draw a pension – in full or in part. In theory, at least, directors can now step down gradually and carry on in a part-time capacity, perhaps as a non-executive.

Such flexibility is only possible if your scheme allows it, and many defined benefit schemes have now changed their rules, particularly in the light of age discrimination legislation.

All benefits must be in payment by the time you reach 75.

Minimum retirement age

The earliest age at which most people can draw their pension will officially increase to 55 (from 50) by 2010. Some schemes may introduce the requirement earlier; the trustees will need to keep you informed.

You will still be able to get benefits before you reach 55 if:

☐ you are eligible for an ill-health or incapacity pension. (The rules for this are fairly prescriptive and will be set out in the pension scheme booklet.)

☐ you had the right to do so under the terms of your pension scheme, and the right was documented before December 10, 2003. (If you exercise this right, you will need to take all of your benefits at the same time and leave employment completely.)

People in certain occupations, such as sport, are allowed, as a result of a special concession by H M Revenue and Customs, to retire before 50. The lifetime allowance will be reduced by 2.5 per cent for each year that the person takes the pension before 50.

Generally, retirement before the age of 55 will only be practically possible for those people who have other savings.

Tax-free cash payment

It is possible to take up to a quarter of your pension fund (including any additional contributions you have paid) as a tax-free cash payment.

Membership of more than one pension scheme

You are able to join more than one registered pension scheme at the same time – in fact, you are able to join as many as you want. Annual tax relief will be given on the higher of £3,600 (the threshold for total yearly contributions to pension schemes) and your UK earnings (subject to the overall annual allowance limit of £225,000 for 2007/8).

Income drawdown

Ten years ago, a member of a personal pension plan or a defined contribution scheme had no option but to buy an **annuity** on retirement.

An annuity is a product, usually sold by insurance companies, that promises a certain income until death. What you get therefore depends on how expensive annuities are at the time you retire. Whether they are good value depends on how long you live. If you live a long time, you will do very well. Some people, however, do not survive long after retirement and so do not do so well (even if their wife, husband or partner gets a pension after their death). It is all a bit of a gamble.

Not surprisingly, annuities have been unpopular with retirees. To make things fairer, the government introduced what is known as **income drawdown**. Income drawdown allows the retiring member to put off buying an annuity and take some of their pension pot as income each year.

You do not need to buy an annuity when you reach 75. Instead, you will be able to buy what is known as an **alternatively secured pension** (ASP), which allows you to continue drawing income from your pension pot but in a reduced amount once you are 75. This helps to ensure the funds are not used up too quickly.

However, the government was concerned that some people saw an ASP as a good way to accumulate capital rather than as an alternative to an annuity. In December 2006, therefore, it announced changes to ensure that ASPs are used to provide an income in retirement and not to pass on capital tax free to dependants.

Income drawdown is a tricky area as the rules are complicated. In addition, you need to have sufficient funds to make the costs worthwhile. And your income will fluctuate in line with the performance of your investments.

If you think income drawdown is for you, seek advice before making a final decision.

6.   Other forms of pension

Small self-administered schemes (SSASs)

SSASs used to be very attractive to controlling directors. They offered a tax-efficient vehicle that allowed directors to be trustees and members of their occupational pension scheme.

Trustee members had control over how the assets were invested, and the restrictions were few.

The relative attractions of SSASs have diminished since April 6, 2006, when all pension schemes became subject to one investment regime. The schemes, however, will not disappear quickly, and will continue to operate for some time.

Executive pension plans (EPPs)

EPPs, when used, were normally set up for directors and senior executives. They are usually contracted into the state scheme and are defined contribution schemes. Like SSASs, they will become less common in future.

Self-invested personal pension plans (SIPPs)

SIPPs are personal pension plans that allow individuals to select their own investments. You must use an external provider to hold the money for you.

SIPPs offer members more control in managing investments and are therefore attractive to sophisticated investors. Investing in residential property, paintings, antiques etc is, however, prohibited.

7.   Pension rights on dismissal

Your pension rights are likely to be found in a number of documents, including those below.

- ☐   **Your service contract:** this should refer to any pension arrangement to which your employer will make contributions. If the arrangement is a personal pension plan or a stakeholder scheme, it will typically give details of the pension provider and the level of contributions. If your company has an occupational scheme, the service contract will probably refer to the pension scheme booklet, where more detailed information can be found. Usually, the contract will give your employer the right to change the pension scheme, either expressly or by invoking the power of amendment in the pension scheme.

☐ **The pension scheme booklet:** the trustees of any occupational pension scheme are required by law to give you certain details about the scheme. These include an outline of how to join, the benefits available, how much you will need to contribute and how to make a complaint.

If you are made **redundant or are asked to leave your company** you may be entitled to compensation. Your rights will depend on your circumstances and what your service agreement says (see chapter 4). You should always seek legal advice.

In summary, you are entitled to be put back into the position you would have been in had your service agreement been properly complied with. So, if you are over 50 (55 from 2010) this may mean that you should be retiring on pension.

If you are a member of a personal pension, stakeholder or defined contribution scheme you should be entitled to compensation for lost pension contributions during **any**

CASE NOTES: CLARK V BET

John Clark was the chief executive and managing director of the facilities management company BET (formerly known as British Electric Traction). He had a three-year notice period.

In 1996, BET was taken over by rival company Rentokil, and the 55-year-old Clark was fired without notice – i.e. wrongfully dismissed. Clark sued BET for damages.

A provision in Clark's defined benefit pension scheme allowed him to take immediate retirement on an unreduced pension if he were made redundant after a takeover. This meant Clark's pension rights at 55 were more valuable than they would have been if he had retired at the end of his notice period. (Usually, pensions are reduced to take account of early payment.)

Clark was entitled to receive the pension unreduced at 55. His compensation award was not lowered to take this increased pension into account. He was also entitled to claim for pension loss. The pension loss alone was worth £550,000.

period of notice. This loss will be reduced to reflect the fact that you will be receiving the contributions as a single lump sum rather than over a period of time.

If you are a member of a defined benefit scheme the position is more complicated. To calculate your pension loss, you need to look at your pension rights at the date you leave and the pension rights you would have had at the end of your notice period. The difference is the pension loss. An actuary will have to calculate the value of this difference, unless you are offered an additional period of service in the pension scheme to cover the notice period. Several factors will need to be taken into account. They include:

☐ any pay rises you might have been entitled to during your notice period;

☐ the fact that you are being paid the money before you would have been entitled to it;

☐ any new job you may get, as this is likely to offer some form of pension;

☐ any contributions that you would have had to make during the notice period.

If you are entitled to a pension when you leave employment, your employer is not allowed to take any pension benefits that you receive during your notice period into account when calculating compensation for the loss of your job. This is the case even if you receive an enhanced pension under the pension scheme rules on dismissal or redundancy. What is more, if your pension at the end of your notice period is less than it would have been had you been allowed to serve out your notice, you may claim for pension loss without any adjustment for the pension payments you receive in the meantime. (The short case study shown on page 107, Clark v BET, helps to explain these rules.)

Part II: A trustee's duties

1.   Introduction

Directors often have an interest in pensions that goes beyond their interest in their own pension entitlement. Many are trustees of the company pension scheme. This inevitably means additional duties and additional risks. Often the implications are not fully appreciated when the appointment is offered and accepted.

The risks can be extreme. In one of the leading trust law cases, a set of trustees acted in accordance with advice received from a leading barrister about their duties. An aggrieved beneficiary complained, and the matter ultimately reached the House of Lords, who by a three to two majority agreed with the beneficiary. As a result, the trustees were ordered to repay millions to the trust. One of the trustees committed suicide in the face of bankruptcy.

Although such an outcome is highly unusual – it is rare to hear of trustees being sued in a personal capacity – the possibility exists. Trusteeship is not a role to take lightly, and you should think carefully before accepting the appointment.

2. The nature of trusteeship

The trustees hold the legal title of the pension scheme assets and have stringent legal duties to ensure that those assets are used to provide benefits in accordance with the terms of the trust (as overridden by statute).

Essentially, a pension scheme trustee's duties are to:

☐   hold the trust assets;

☐   invest the assets in accordance with the terms of the trust, and prudently;

☐   collect the contributions as required by the terms of the trust;

☐   pay the benefits in accordance with the terms of the trust.

Trustees are also legally required to be familiar with the pension scheme's documentation and have an understanding of the legal, funding and investment obligations relating to the scheme. They will need to keep records to show the regulator that they have complied.

Essentially, the legal requirements mean that you should read the trust deed and rules of the pension scheme carefully before becoming a trustee. While most trust deeds are not exactly page-turners, this is an effort well worth making.

If you do not understand anything, ask questions. You would be surprised how often the wording is out of date, ambiguous or just plain wrong. Since statute often overrides the terms of the trust, you should make sure you get trustee training, and legal advice where necessary.

Every pension lawyer will advise you to take these steps, and every pension lawyer will concede that most clients take no notice. The late libel lawyer Peter Carter-Ruck was heard frequently to observe that he ran his office off the clients who took his advice and his Rolls-Royce off the clients who did not. The same observation could be made, on this point at least, about pension lawyers.

3. Personal liability

Forms of protection

As noted above, trustees potentially put everything on the line. To what extent can they protect themselves?

There are three different types of protection available to trustees: indemnities, insurance and exoneration clauses. An **indemnity**, whether contained in a trust deed or in a side-letter, acknowledges that a third party (whether the pension scheme or the employer or some other party) will ensure that a trustee is not out of pocket if he or she is found liable in given circumstances. By this analysis, **trustee insurance** is effectively just another form of indemnity.

The concept of indemnities will be relatively familiar to directors, exoneration clauses less so. Trustees benefit from a **statutory exoneration** under section 61 of the Trustee Act 1925, which says that if it appears to the court that a trustee is personally liable for any breach of trust, but has acted honestly and reasonably, and ought fairly to be excused, then the court may relieve him or her from personal liability. The problem is that this provision does not automatically apply. It is only effective if a particular court, in its discretion, decides to make use of it.

Additionally, trustees may have the benefit of express **exoneration provisions in the pension scheme rules**. However, the courts will not interpret such clauses as allowing trustees to act in bad faith or recklessly. Trustees who think they can get away with anything because they are protected by the exoneration clause are likely to have a rude awakening.

An exoneration clause does not prevent the pensions regulator from imposing a fine for breach of one of the particular statutory provisions over which it has control. Fines by the pensions regulator, however, are rare and can only apply where trustees have failed to take "all such steps as are reasonable to secure compliance" with the particular statutory duty.

Under section 33 of the Pensions Act 1995, exoneration provisions do not apply to trustees in relation to the performance of their investment functions. But if trustees delegate decisions about investments to a **fund manager**, they will not be responsible for any defaults by that fund manager if they have taken all reasonable steps to ensure that he or she:

☐ has the appropriate knowledge and experience for managing the scheme investments;

☐ carries out his or her work competently; and

☐ has regard to the need for proper diversification of investments.

Limits to protection

Indemnities and exoneration clauses can have substantially different effects. An indemnity (or insurance) is only as good as the person who undertakes to pay out. Where the indemnifier does not have funds to meet the indemnity, it is useless. Where the indemnifier is unwilling to pay out, the trustees may find themselves in serious difficulties and may need to take legal action to recover the money. An exoneration clause, on the other hand, requires no action by the trustees. The beneficiary seeking to claim against the trustee will be unable to succeed because the trustee will not be liable. Exoneration clauses, however, will only protect you against claims by members or the employer. They will not help if your investment managers, for example, make a claim.

From the viewpoint of members, indemnities are often seen as more desirable than exoneration clauses: exoneration clauses can leave schemes seriously out of pocket for the mistakes of trustees.

Trustee indemnity insurance can potentially give added protection to the trustees if they cannot rely on their indemnity protection. The insurance may reimburse the trustees for any successful claim brought against them by a beneficiary.

Trustees should bear in mind that this type of insurance cover is normally heavily skewed in favour of the insurer. Insurers have almost never made a payment to trustees under an indemnity insurance policy. It is very important for the trustees to seek to ensure that any claims against them are not upheld in the first place by administering the scheme properly and ensuring that they are happy with the exoneration provisions – prevention is far better than cure.

5. Corporate trustees

There is no rule of law that says that trustees need to be individuals. It is entirely possible to have a company as a trustee, and many pension schemes operate in this way, with the individuals who would have been trustees acting as directors of the trustee company. This has significant advantages for the trustee directors, though it has some drawbacks also. The chief advantage is that it is the company that is liable to scheme members, not the trustee directors. The trustee directors' only duties are to the trustee company. The duties of a director are a little less exacting than the duties of a trustee (although as this book shows, they are still demanding).

Pension scheme members can still enforce duties owed by a trustee director through what is known as a "dog leg" claim (it is the director who takes the role of the lamp post). But in order to do this, the member must first show that the trustee company breached its duties to the pension scheme, and secondly that the trustee director breached their duties to the company. It is harder to show two breaches of duty than one.

The chief disadvantage is that company law is much more restrictive than trust law about the extent to which directors can be indemnified or exonerated by the companies of which they are a director (see section 14 of chapter 7).

6.   Conflicts of interest

Trustees should exercise their powers in order to further the purposes of the pension scheme. The courts have developed strict tests to ensure that trustees do this. One of the duties of trustees is not to put themselves in a position where there is a conflict between their duties as a trustee and their private interests. The court will not consider whether or not the trustee has allowed their external interest to influence the decision-making – the fact that he or she has acted while in a position of conflict of interest will be enough to constitute a breach of trust.

For directors, this can be a particularly difficult problem. If a director is a trustee and a member of the pension scheme, on any given issue they may have multiple competing interests (for example, the setting of employer contribution rates at a time when company finances are hard-pressed).

The problem has been addressed in part by statute, and the courts have also set out a limited exception to the strict conflict of interest rule. Neither of these changes offers a complete solution to the problems of directors: extreme care still needs to be taken.

When the government introduced what was to become the **Pensions Act 1995**, a central feature was the drive for pension schemes to have **member-nominated trustees**. The government recognised that members would frequently have theoretical conflicts between their personal interests and their duties as trustees. Section 39 of the Pensions Act 1995 therefore gives protection to trustees who are also members of the pension scheme.

This is less helpful than it may appear. It applies only to a member's interest as a member. A trustee who owes director's duties to the employer would not be able to rely upon the terms of section 39. Also, trustees must still exercise their powers in order to further the purposes of the pension scheme. Trustees who act in their own interests and against the interests of the scheme will find themselves in deep trouble.

Separately, the courts have also been looking to the commercial realities of pension scheme trusteeship and showing a markedly more sympathetic approach. The Court of Appeal considered the problem in *Edge v Pensions Ombudsman*, where the pension scheme rules required the trustees to hold or have held an office equivalent to that of director. The court recognised that decisions of such trustees would inevitably be perceived by some to favour one interest at the expense of another. The court concluded that the only sensible answer was to accept that the scheme was established on the basis that the pension rules were intended to provide a body of trustees that could be relied upon to consider all interests fairly and properly; and that those who seek to challenge a decision of that body should bear the ordinary burden of establishing that the decision has been reached improperly.

If your pension scheme rules specify the composition of the trustee body, this ruling could come to your assistance in cases where the conflict between the different duties is slight.

Of course, there are occasions where your interests and duties conflict starkly. Just how should you approach the setting of employer contribution rates at a time when company finances are hard-pressed? The company's and the pension scheme's interests may be diametrically opposed. As a director, you owe duties to both. If you find yourself in such a conflict, you should take legal advice as to whether you need to step aside from the decision-making process, or even resign one of your offices.

Between the cases where the conflict is slight (for example, deciding whether to grant a small increase to all members' benefits, including your own) and the cases where the conflict is extreme, there are intermediate cases. How should you decide whether you can safely act or not? There is a simple rule of thumb: if you find yourself badly wanting to be involved in the decision, you should probably stand aside.

7. Confidentiality of information

A related topic is the subject of confidential information. Trustees are obliged to use all information at their disposal when considering trustee business. It may well be that with other hats on you are aware of relevant information. You are obliged to use that information, and to share it with your co-trustees, if it has the potential to affect decision-making.

But what if that information is confidential? The simplest solution is to persuade the company to allow you to release the information to your co-trustees "for their eyes only", but that may not always be possible. If it is not, you should take legal advice without delay.

8. Giving advice to employees

There are specific statutory obligations relating to the disclosure of information, which your pensions advisers can help you with. But perhaps surprisingly, neither trustees nor employers are under any general legal duty to advise pension scheme members about their pension rights.

In fact, it is good practice not to advise members about their rights at all. It is all too easy to fall into the trap of giving advice of the type that is regulated by the Financial Services Authority (which most directors and trustees are not authorised to give). Still more dangerously, you could run the risk of giving the wrong advice because you do not know all of the facts. Employees may keep crucial bits of information about their personal circumstances hidden from you – for example, the fact that they are about to hand in their notice.

Sometimes the advice could run directly counter to the interests of other members. Trustees should not favour one group at the expense of another group.

The best policy, despite the natural human instinct to be helpful, is therefore to avoid giving advice to pension scheme members, no matter how much they look for a steer from you. And do not make the mistake of giving advice "off the record" – you are just as liable for off the record advice as you are for on the record advice.

Part III: Liabilities for underfunding

1. Introduction

Defined benefit schemes can sometimes hit funding problems. At the moment, though, there is, as stated in part I, no legal requirement for an employer to fund its defined benefit scheme at a level that guarantees all the benefits at all times. There will be enough money to pay benefits as they fall due while the scheme is "live". If, however, the scheme is wound up, there may be a problem.

In June 2003 (in response to a rising panic that employers were deserting their defined benefit pension schemes in droves, leaving insufficient money to pay for all the benefits), the government announced that any employer that wound up its scheme would have to top it up until it could secure all members' benefits in full with an insurance company. This is called "funding on the buy-out basis" and is at present very expensive. (See 4 below, final paragraph.)

The government also worried that employers would rearrange their affairs to avoid this buy-out debt. It therefore gave the new pensions regulator sweeping powers to bring errant companies into line. In theory, at least, no attempt to evade pension liabilities will go unnoticed. The regulator's powers are listed in section 2 below.

Directors should take underfunding very seriously. It is not something that will go away by itself and could well take up a significant amount of management time. It could also cost the company a lot of money and, in some circumstances, even bring the business down.

2. The regulator's powers

☐ **Contribution notices:** the regulator is able to recover (where reasonable) a sum up to the full statutory debt from one or more persons (or companies) who were involved in an act – or a failure to act – that had as its main purpose the avoidance of pension liabilities. Any acts or omissions since April 26, 2004 can be investigated.

☐ **Financial support directions:** if the regulator considers that the pension scheme employer is insufficiently resourced to pay any debt that may arise, it is able to issue a financial support direction against other companies in the group.

☐ **Restoration order:** where money or property has been transferred out of a pension scheme at an undervalue in the two years before an insolvency event or application for protection from the pension protection fund, the regulator can order its return.

Anyone who may be subject to either a contribution notice or a financial support direction will be able to seek a clearance statement from the regulator. This, however, will not guarantee impunity. (See section 4, below.)

3.   The position of individual directors

The regulator does not have the power to make a financial support direction against an individual unless the employer is a sole trader or a partnership.

It does, though, have wide powers to impose contribution notices against individuals. To be caught, you need to be "connected" or "associated" with an employer in the pension scheme. Connected or associated in this context is very widely defined. Any director or employee could be caught, but shareholders are exempt unless they "control" the company – i.e. own at least one third of the voting shares. Shareholders can also be caught if they and someone associated or connected with them (for example, a spouse) own one third of the shares together.

4.   Reducing the risk of personal liability

There are several things you could do to reduce the likelihood of action by the regulator.

☐   **Request a clearance statement from the regulator**

The regulator expects clearance to be sought only when a particular action is financially detrimental to the ability of a defined benefit pension scheme to meet its liabilities. This means that the scheme must be in deficit and the triggering event must fall within certain categories that are listed by the pensions regulator in its published guidance. Any clearance will apply until there is a "material change in circumstances". The consequences of this remain unclear; it could, though, reduce the usefulness of the clearance statement.

☐   **Take advice**

The regulator can only make a contribution notice against you if it is reasonable to do so. It will need to look at your financial circumstances, the purpose of the act complained of (for example, to limit the loss of employment) and your involvement in the scheme or failure. If you are contemplating doing anything that may result in pension scheme liabilities being avoided you should be sure to seek legal advice first.

Companies should also take their own advice as soon as possible. Trustees of the pension scheme will probably have already consulted their actuarial (and possibly legal) advisers and are likely to demand more money from the company. The company may be able to negotiate with the trustees, but this will depend on its financial position, the extent of the underfunding and the terms of the pension scheme itself.

Professional advisers will be familiar with the issues involved and will be able to suggest ways of managing the underfunding to fit in with the circumstances of your company. The company should speak to professionals such as actuaries, legal advisers and benefit consultants.

Given that the exercise can take up a lot of management time, it may be worth putting together a small, dedicated team to look at the issue and keep the rest of the board informed. Such a team would obviously need to include the finance director.

☐ Talk to the trustees

The trustees will be concerned to put any underfunding in the pension scheme right. They have duties to the members; and they have statutory duties to report underfunding or non-payment of contributions to the pensions regulator. Equally, they will not want to push the company into insolvency as that would mean job losses (and will also make it more difficult to get any money out of the company).

The amount that the trustees can ask for will be governed both by legislation and by the documentation of the pension scheme itself. Legislation requires defined benefit schemes to be funded in accordance with the "statutory funding objective". This is a scheme-specific system, which the trustees must agree with the employer. The process for setting it is fairly prescriptive, and the pensions regulator has issued detailed guidance about what it expects. These funding requirements are fairly new – they only became effective in December 2005 – and some schemes at the time of writing (March 2007) have yet to use them. They are, however, already resulting in schemes being better funded.

The trustees have a lot of power in the process of making sure funding requirements are met.

☐ Find out if you need to contact the pensions regulator

Since May 2005, trustees, employers and other professional advisers involved in the pension scheme have had to notify the pensions regulator of certain matters. Failure to do so could leave the offender liable to a civil fine. Issues that need to be notified by employers are wide-ranging and include any decision to compromise a debt, any breach of the employer's banking covenant and a significant change in the employer's credit rating.

☐ Be careful not to wind up the pension scheme by mistake

Getting rid of the pension scheme may look like an attractive option. But if the scheme winds up (either by accident or design), the companies participating in it will be liable for the buy-out debt. The amount of this debt can be very high: the scheme will need to be funded to a level where the benefits of all members can be secured with annuities bought from insurance companies; at the time of writing (March 2007), annuities are substantially more expensive than the standard terms for valuing benefits in pension schemes.

Buy-out debt will often push a company into insolvency. Sometimes (but not always), trustees will agree to a lower payment by the company if they believe that they will get more if the company continues than if it is wound up. However, the pensions regulator will need to be involved in any such agreement. Again, seeking advice early should help to avoid winding-up happening by mistake.

remuneration issues

CHAPTER 6

1. Introduction

As chapter 4 made clear, the remuneration of directors remains a "hot" business topic, with companies under increased pressure to get it "right". Pay policies must not only attract and retain the best executive talent but also be fair and justifiable.

The **2002 Directors' Remuneration Report Regulations ("the Regulations")** extended the power of shareholders, entitling them to an advisory vote on the remuneration report at each annual general meeting. The **2003 Higgs review** on the role and effectiveness of non-executives (see chapter 3) led to changes to sections in the Combined Code dealing with remuneration.

UK institutional investors have been swift to respond to the new regulatory environment. The annual vote on remuneration reports has given them an opportunity to comment each year on those aspects of companies' remuneration that do not meet their views of what is acceptable good practice. Since these views evolve over time, remuneration committees now need to consider each year whether their policies remain appropriate.

As well as demands from the government, the UK Listing Authority and investor bodies, companies, of course, have the media to deal with. Clashes between investors and companies make good stories. Get remuneration wrong and your public, your customers, will soon hear about it.

The environment, though, is not all bad from a company's perspective. Many companies have used the new regulatory framework as an opportunity to engage with institutional shareholders and to demonstrate how remuneration policies fit within broader and changing company strategies. As a consequence of improved dialogue with shareholders, some are able to achieve "bespoke" remuneration arrangements that fit their specific outlook and circumstances.

The guidelines of institutional investors are not rigid: there is room for flexibility, if a good case can be made.

While headline-grabbing cases of "no votes" are likely to continue, they are far from the norm. For every United Business Media or Amvescap (see box next page), there are many other companies that successfully review remuneration arrangements ahead of the AGM. Research by Deloitte, published by the DTI in January 2005, found not only a significant increase in compliance with the Regulations but also evidence of better investor relations: more than 90 per cent of shareholders said communications with companies had improved.

SHAREHOLDER POWER OVER PAY: UNITED BUSINESS MEDIA

Although the shareholder vote on the remuneration report, compulsory since 2003, is only advisory it can have a powerful impact. This was demonstrated in May 2005 by investors in publishing group United Business Media.

The annual remuneration report disclosed the payment of a special £250,000 bonus to the company's chief executive Lord Hollick for ensuring a successful handover to the new chief executive David Levin. This triggered a major rebellion, with 76 per cent of shareholders voting **against** the 2004 remuneration report at the AGM.

UBM claimed it was contractually bound to pay the bonus whatever shareholders said, and Lord Hollick appeared defiant, saying he had earned the money. The shareholders protested that ensuring a smooth transition was one of the "normal duties" of a chief executive and did not merit a special award.

Peter Montagnon, head of investment affairs at the Association of British Insurers (ABI), the voice of some of the UK's biggest institutional investors, was quoted in the *Financial Times* of May 13, 2005 as saying: "The company's owners have spoken. If Lord Hollick insists on keeping the payment then he will be remembered for defying 76 per cent of shareholders – and not for his good performance as chief executive."

A few days later, Lord Hollick agreed to waive his right to receive the money.

Since the UBM case, builders' merchants Travis Perkins and fund management group Amvescap have both been subject to shareholder revolts over "handover" bonuses. Although Amvescap did have its remuneration report approved in 2006, only 51 per cent of shareholders were in favour.

This chapter aims to give a practical guide to setting remuneration policy. It examines some of the key issues companies face when trying to devise packages that are cost-effective and "efficient" and that please both beneficiaries and shareholders.

2. Reference points

Employers in general – and quoted companies in particular – should today be aware of the following when setting pay policies:

☐ the **Combined Code on Corporate Governance**, particularly Section 1B (remuneration) and Schedule A (provisions on the design of performance related remuneration);

☐ the **Financial Services Authority's Listing Rules**, particularly LR 9.8.8 (relating to disclosure of directors' remuneration) and LR 9.4 and LR 13.8.11 to 13.8.15 (relating to approval of share plans by shareholders);

☐ **the Companies Act** and regulations made under it that legislate for the contents of the directors' remuneration report for quoted companies, as well as setting out the basic remuneration disclosure requirements for all companies, quoted and unquoted;

☐ **the guidelines of UK institutional investor bodies**, particularly those of the Association of British Insurers or ABI ("Executive Remuneration – ABI Guidelines on Policies and Practices") and the National Association of Pension Funds or NAPF ("Corporate Governance Policy").

3.   Remuneration and unquoted companies

The main focus of this chapter is quoted companies and, principally, fully quoted companies rather than those with shares traded on the Alternative Investment Market (AIM).

However, some of the issues covered will be common to all companies. What level of shareholder dilution is acceptable for share plans? What should annual bonus performance targets be? These questions can be universal.

Also, the system and procedures for deciding remuneration can be the same in a private company as they are in a public one. An unquoted company, may, for example, set up a separate remuneration committee involving non-executive directors. In some cases, the practice will be imported by investors and non-executives who join the business from a public-company background. In others, it will result from a desire to demonstrate good governance practice to potential outside investors.

The position of AIM companies is illustrative. AIM companies are not quoted companies for these purposes, and therefore do not have to comply with the disclosure requirements for quoted companies' remuneration reports or to put such reports to a vote of shareholders; AIM companies are not subject to the Combined Code; the AIM rules do not require companies to seek shareholders' approval to establish new share plans. However, many AIM companies:

☐ make much fuller disclosure on remuneration than is required under the Companies Act and will produce a separate remuneration report within their annual report and accounts;

☐ voluntarily adopt some of the Combined Code's recommendations, having, for example, remuneration committees made up of independent non-executives;

☐ frequently model their share plans on share plans for fully quoted companies, particularly with regard to performance conditions, dilution capacity, limits on individual awards and the requirement to seek shareholders' approval for changes that benefit participants.

4. Deciding remuneration packages

Best practice; the remuneration committee

Principle B.2 of the Combined Code states that:

"There should be a formal and transparent procedure for developing policy on executive remuneration and for fixing the remuneration packages of individual directors. No director should be involved in deciding his or her own remuneration."

Quoted companies fulfil this obligation by having a remuneration committee.

Committee membership

According to provision B.2.1 of the Code, remuneration committees should have "at least three, or in the case of smaller companies two, members who should all be independent non-executive directors".

A smaller company is a company outside the FTSE 350. The Combined Code's tests of "independence" are discussed in chapter 3 on corporate governance.

Since June 2006, the Combined Code has accepted that a company chairman may sit on, but not chair, the remuneration committee if he or she was considered independent on appointment as chairman.

The committee's terms of reference

Remuneration committees must, says the Combined Code, make their terms of reference publicly available – an obligation usually fulfilled via the company's website. The Institute of Chartered Secretaries (ICSA), which helped compile a list of the principal duties of the remuneration committee for the Higgs review, has published guidance notes giving model terms of reference. These can be downloaded from its website.

Central to the role of the "remco" is the concept of **delegated responsibility**. As seen in section 14 of chapter 3, the terms of reference must make clear that committee members actually set the remuneration for all executive directors and the chairman; their role is not merely to make suggestions.

Furthermore, the influence of the committee extends beyond the pay of the boardroom. Code provision B.2.2. says:

"The committee should also recommend and monitor the level and structure of remuneration for senior management."

The Code's expectation is that senior management for this purpose should normally include the first layer of management below board level.

The ABI's guidelines say that remuneration committees should pay particular attention to arrangements for those senior executives who are not board members but who have a significant influence over the company's ability to meet its strategic targets.

However, the most recent version of the ABI guidelines (December 2006) has dropped a previous request for disclosure of the remuneration for these executives in companies' remuneration reports. Nonetheless, International Accounting Standard 24 ("Related Party Transactions") requires the disclosure of some details of their remuneration in companies' reports and accounts, but on an aggregated basis with remuneration paid to directors.

Appointment of remuneration consultants

The Combined Code (supporting principle B.2) says that remuneration committees should be responsible for any appointment of consultants "in respect of executive director remuneration". It also says (B.2.1) that the company must state publicly (again via its website) whether the appointed consultants have any other connections with the company.

These points are echoed in – and given more force by – the Regulations, which require the committee to disclose in the remuneration report:

☐ the name of any person who assisted it in the consideration of any matter (this applies not only to external advisers but also to internal company officers such as senior HR executives);

☐ whether that person provided any other services to the company during the relevant financial year;

☐ whether that person was appointed by the committee.

5. Institutional investors

The ABI and the NAPF

The representatives of the big UK shareholders have a long-standing policy of engaging with companies when it comes to their remuneration practices.

The ABI's **"Executive Remuneration – ABI Guidelines on Policies and Practices"** reflects the views of its members on features of remuneration practice. The guidelines have been annually updated in recent years, and therefore provide a good insight into developing views among institutional investors. Initially focusing on share plan design, they have, over recent years, been extended to cover the responsibilities of remuneration committees, base pay, annual bonuses, pensions and service contracts.

The ABI also runs a comprehensive monitoring service – the **Institutional Voting Information Service (IVIS)**. IVIS reviews the remuneration reports and AGM proposals for share plans of every FTSE All-Share company and produces a report that is available to subscribers. It also reports on general Combined Code compliance. The service is widely taken by institutional investors.

IVIS operates a colour coding system for companies:

- ☐ **blue top** – complies with ABI guidelines and corporate governance best practice;

- ☐ **amber top** – gives cause for concern;

- ☐ **red top** – non-compliant or inconsistent with guidelines, resulting in a decision by members to abstain or vote against;

- ☐ **green top** – previously reported as inconsistent or non-compliant but the problem is now resolved.

The **NAPF** is also an important body, particularly since the launch of its monitoring service, **Research Recommendations Electronic Voting (RREV)** in 2004. RREV has a similar coverage to IVIS (FTSE All-Share) and produces reports on companies' governance and remuneration practices, with AGM voting recommendations.

RREV is a joint venture between NAPF and an American proxy voting information service, Institutional Shareholder Services (ISS). ISS's recommendations are widely followed by US institutional investors. Consequently, a favourable report from RREV will be important in securing the support of any US institutional investors for remuneration report votes or AGM share plan proposals.

THE ABI'S 2006 GUIDELINES

In response to criticism that its guidelines had become impenetrable for companies and were essentially a "practitioners' document", the ABI substantially re-styled them in December 2006. The new format mirrors that used by the Combined Code. It features:

☐ five key principles;

☐ 17 main provisions; and

☐ detailed guidance supporting the 17 main provisions.

None of the five key principles is new. Each is set out in full below.

☐ Boards are responsible for adopting remuneration policies and practices that promote the success of companies in creating value for shareholders over the longer term. The policies and practices should be demonstrably aligned with the corporate objectives and business strategy, and they should be reviewed regularly.

☐ Remuneration committees should be established in accordance with the provisions of the Combined Code. They should comprise independent directors who bring independent thought and scrutiny to all aspects of remuneration. It is important to maintain a constructive and timely dialogue between boards and shareholders regarding remuneration policies and practices.

☐ Executive remuneration should be set at levels that retain and motivate, based on selection and interpretation of appropriate benchmarks. Such benchmarks should be used with caution, in view of the risk of an upward ratcheting of remuneration levels with no corresponding improvement in performance.

☐ Executive remuneration should be linked to individual and corporate performance through graduated targets, which align the interests of executives with those of shareholders. The resulting arrangements should be clear and readily understandable.

☐ Shareholders will not support arrangements that entitle executives to reward when this is not justified by performance. Remuneration committees should ensure that service contracts contain provisions that are consistent with this principle.

The NAPF also produces its own "Corporate Governance Policy". In places, this has a different emphasis from the ABI's guidelines.

PIRC

A further monitoring service on governance and remuneration matters is provided by Pensions and Investment Research Consultants (PIRC). PIRC is an independent organisation but its reports are taken by a number of institutional investors and its recommendations frequently attract press attention. The service is designed to help institutional investors make "considered use" of their votes.

Individual institutions

Individual institutions tend to have marked preferences in relation to certain aspects of remuneration practice. For example, some greatly prefer one form of performance condition for long-term incentives to another.

This means that it is often not enough to talk to a representative body when trying to establish your shareholders' views on remuneration. Or simply to refer to published ABI and NAPF guidelines. In many cases, you need also to approach the individual corporate governance officers at the relevant institutions.

Consultation

ABI guidelines give a very clear endorsement to the growing practice of informally consulting shareholders about any proposed changes to a company's remuneration practice.

CONSULTING INSTITUTIONAL SHAREHOLDERS: A BRIEF GUIDE

Timing – the consultation should normally take place in **advance** of the publication of a remuneration report and/or AGM shareholders' circular in which a company would be required to set out its proposals formally. This gives institutions an opportunity to comment on proposals and (if appropriate) for the company to make any modifications to secure shareholder support.

Method – the process should be initiated by the company (normally in the shape of the remuneration committee chairman) writing to major shareholders. The letter will outline the main aspects of the proposals (for example, performance conditions, dilution impacts, the level of individual awards). The letter should set a deadline for responses and also give contact points for queries – the remuneration committee chairman, a company officer familiar with the proposals such as the company secretary or, sometimes, an external adviser. Some consultations can be more intensive and involve a "roadshow" presentation for investors.

Scope – cases vary, but companies typically consult their leading 10 or so institutional investors, and any other investors that they regard as having an interest above a significant threshold (e.g. one per cent or 1.5 per cent of issued share capital). In addition, a company should probably include any investors who have previously commented on the company's remuneration practices, even if they are outside the parameters set for the consultation. Companies will also generally consult the ABI and NAPF/RREV or at least make them aware that a consultation with individual investors is in progress.

The ABI will itself play an important role in the exercise – through giving its own views on proposals and (when asked to do so) through co-ordinating the responses of interested ABI members.

The box on page 127 gives further information on how the process of informal consultation usually works.

6.   Design of remuneration packages

This section considers some of the approaches companies take to the design of base salary, benefits, annual bonuses and pensions. Share incentives are considered in the next section.

"Total remuneration" and the "balance" of the package

Many companies look at packages on a "total remuneration" basis – that is, they consider all the elements of an executive's package together, rather than each one (base salary, benefits, pension entitlements, annual bonus and share incentives) in isolation.

In theory, this allows them to compare the "total value" of remuneration packages in their sector or market. But, while useful, a total remuneration analysis can only be an approximate guide. The differences between the separate elements of remuneration packages can make like-for-like comparisons difficult. One company may, for example, offer an expensive final salary pension plan; another, a money purchase plan.

An alternative approach is to focus on the "balance" within a package between the fixed elements (base salary, benefits, pensions) and the variable or performance-linked elements (annual bonus, share incentives). The balance of a package is given emphasis in both the Combined Code and the ABI guidelines.

Principle B.1 of the Combined Code states:

"Levels of remuneration should be sufficient to attract, retain and motivate directors of the quality required to run the company successfully, but a company should avoid paying more than is necessary for this purpose. A significant proportion of executive directors' remuneration should be structured so as to link rewards to corporate and individual performance."

The ABI's guidelines for the structure of remuneration say:

"Remuneration committees are responsible for ensuring that the mix of incentives reflects the company's needs, establishes an appropriate balance between fixed and variable remuneration, and is based on targets that are stretching, verifiable and relevant."

The government seems to concur with these views. Under the Regulations, a quoted company must disclose the relative importance of performance-linked and non-performance-linked elements of remuneration. Many companies fulfil this disclosure requirement by including in the policy section of their remuneration report a form of "boilerplate" that tracks the wording of the Code closely – for example: "a significant proportion of directors' remuneration is performance-linked through participation in the annual bonus plan and share incentive plans". Others go further, using graphs to illustrate the relative importance of the elements of a director's remuneration. An example would be a bar chart showing a split between salary (40 per cent), target annual bonus (30 per cent) and expected long-term share incentives (30 per cent). An interesting development in relation to companies' disclosures of the balance of packages is that investors have begun to ask for pensions to be included in this analysis – this reflects the growing awareness among investors of the value (and cost) of pension arrangements.

Base salary

Base salary remains the foundation stone of remuneration packages, often determining the levels of other elements such as pensions and bonuses.

When setting base salaries for executive directors, companies typically bear in mind:

☐ the director's performance, individual responsibilities and experience;

☐ comparisons with salary levels in other companies.

The former is the more important criterion. While external comparisons can be a useful "benchmark", they should never be used as the sole justification for salary levels. Indeed, the "bandwagon" argument will always be difficult to sell to investors. This is evident from the Combined Code, where the supporting principle to B1 says:

"The remuneration committee should judge where to position their company relative to other companies. But they should use such comparisons with caution, in view of the risk of an upward ratchet of remuneration levels with no corresponding improvement in performance."

This statement has been followed in the ABI's "Key Principles" (see the box on page 126).

When looking at salary data, remuneration committees should ask:

☐   how appropriate are the comparator companies? Should a broader cross-sectoral group of companies with similar market capitalisation and turnover be considered as a "health-check"?

☐   how large is the salary comparator group? Could removing or adding, say, one or two companies significantly alter a quartile analysis?

☐   how up-to-date is the data? Could there have been intervening salary reviews? Has the data been "aged" to reflect possible earnings inflation? Is the ageing factor appropriate?

Since the introduction of the annual vote on remuneration reports, institutional shareholders have been more inclined to comment on base salary rises for executive directors if they view them as out of line with "market norms". This should be remembered in informal discussions about remuneration policy proposals. Agreement on changes to annual bonus schemes and share incentives can count for little if shareholders rebel when details of a base salary rise emerge in the annual report and accounts.

Benefits

With the exception of permanent health insurance (see section 6 of chapter 4) benefits are typically non-contentious. They will usually comprise a mix of insurance benefits and fringe elements or perquisites such as cars and other extras.

Changes to the tax system have led companies to review their approach to benefits. Some now offer a flexible programme whereby employees can choose the things they want from a benefits "menu" – provided, of course, they stick to a budget. Some will offer cash alternatives to company cars.

Annual bonus

The Combined Code's guidance on the design of annual bonus plans is set out in Schedule A, paragraph 1:

"The remuneration committee should consider whether the directors should be eligible for annual bonuses. If so, performance conditions should be relevant, stretching and designed to enhance shareholder value. Upper limits should be set and disclosed. There may be a case for part payment in shares to be held for a significant period."

Typical features of annual bonus plans include:

- ☐ **performance targets** based on internal financial measures (for example, budgeted profits before tax, sales or economic value added), company development measures (for example, product development goals) or personal performance measures (for example, employee safety records);

- ☐ **payments linked to performance targets** – with the maximum made for achievement that exceeds budgeted or predicted levels to a degree specified by the remuneration committee.

Where executives have group-wide responsibilities, the performance targets are likely to focus on group performance. Where executives have distinct divisional responsibilities, the targets will usually be weighted towards divisional performance.

The amount of bonus payable for achieving budgeted or target levels of performance can vary significantly from company to company; it will depend on how stretching the remuneration committee thinks the initial budgeted targets are. For example, some annual bonus plans are structured so that payments are heavily weighted towards achieving the budgeted targets or better. Around half of the maximum may be payable for achieving the budgeted target and only a low level (for example, 10 per cent of the maximum) for near achievement (say, 90 per cent or 95 per cent) of budgeted targets.

Deferral of part or all of a bonus into shares is becoming increasingly common. It is seen by shareholders as a way of aligning directors' interests with theirs; if part of the bonus is delivered in shares after, say, two or three years, the director has a good reason to stay with the company and to improve shareholder returns. (The shares will usually be forfeited if the director leaves during the deferral period.)

Directors will be more ready to accept a deferral if:

- ☐ it is linked to an increase in the overall maximum payment (cash and shares combined);

- ☐ there is an option to accept a lower "cash only" bonus if they need the money.

Unlike long-term share incentive schemes, deferred bonus plans for directors do not need shareholder approval under the Listing Rules, provided they do not involve the issue of new shares.

Companies also get off fairly lightly when it comes to the disclosure rules for bonuses. They must disclose in their annual report and accounts:

☐   any bonuses paid in respect of the financial year;

☐   the bonus maximum for the current financial year.

Other than that, there are no formal requirements – largely because disclosures of performance conditions based on internal budgets could involve the release of commercially sensitive information.

Since the 1995 Greenbury report there has been a best-practice requirement to describe in remuneration reports the types of performance conditions that companies apply to annual bonuses (for example, profits before tax), but not the threshold targets.

Companies need also to be aware of continuing and growing investor interest in bonus-plan design. Institutional shareholders are increasingly asking for additional disclosure for annual bonus performance conditions. The NAPF and ABI have both requested that when bonuses are paid companies disclose in the following year's remuneration report the extent to which target thresholds were achieved.

Annual bonus rises remain an issue of particular concern – since 2003, IVIS has been drawing increases in companies' maximum annual bonus levels to subscribers' attention by giving relevant company reports an "amber top". The 2006 ABI guidelines say that increases in maximum bonus levels should be "explicitly justified" and that shareholders expect increases to be matched by more stretching performance targets.

Pensions

The nature and potential cost of executive directors' pensions has, over recent years, been keeping finance directors awake at night. This is not just because of the much-publicised and continuing "pensions crisis".

There was concern that the increased disclosure requirements for pensions under the Regulations (including disclosure of the total transfer value of an individual director's pension) would be "a story a day" for financial journalists, with large figures providing an easy target. Companies' fears, though, have not been realised. This is probably for two reasons:

☐   pensions disclosures are difficult to understand and to value, particularly on a comparative basis (see above);

☐   there is greater understanding that pensions often represent long-standing contractual promises (particularly in respect of older final salary plans).

Many companies have, nonetheless, been reviewing their pensions arrangements for directors. The principal trigger has been "A day" (April 6, 2006), when the tax regime for pensions was reformed. The focus is, in particular, on those directors who have already accrued tax approved savings above the new tax threshold (or lifetime allowance), set at £1.6m for 2007/8.

Companies have tended to address A day in one of two ways:

- [ ] offering directors the opportunity to continue to accrue pension entitlements, on the understanding that accruals above the lifetime limit will be taxed;

- [ ] offering directors the opportunity to forego further pension accruals and instead accept a "salary supplement" (a fully taxable cash payment) that they can choose to invest in whatever way they want.

Where companies with money-purchase pension plans have offered salary supplements, these are often **lower** than the pension contributions they replace. This is due to the additional employers' National Insurance cost on the cash payments: the company indirectly passes this cost to the director by scaling down the salary supplement so that its overall cost (supplement plus NICs) is not greater than the previous pension contribution cost.

Investor reaction to the post A day environment is, to date, one of "watch this space". The ABI has said that it expects it to take at least two full reporting years for clear post A day market practice to emerge. Accordingly, the ABI's guidelines on what constitutes acceptable practice on executive pensions should be expected to change significantly in coming years.

The ABI's December 2006 guidelines did, however, repeat certain themes that investors have been putting forward for a number of years:

- [ ] disclosures should be full and informative;

- [ ] companies should not compensate individuals for changes in their personal tax position because of A day;

- [ ] companies should consider whether other forms of remuneration could be more "cost-effective than a pension fund and more aligned with shareholder value creation".

More detailed information on pensions and the current tax regime is given in chapter 5.

REWARDING NON-EXECUTIVE DIRECTORS

There have been widespread predictions that non-executive directors' fees will rise significantly to reflect the increasing demands of the role. The Higgs and Smith reports mean greater time commitments and responsibilities (see chapter 3) for non-executives; corporate scandals such as the collapse of Enron and the Conrad Black affair mean greater press scrutiny; and increasing takeover activity, particularly bids from management, places extra burdens on non-executives.

So how should companies decide NEDs' fees?

The key determinants

"Levels of remuneration of non-executive directors should reflect the time commitment and responsibilities of that role" – provision B.1.3 of the Combined Code on Corporate Governance.

Many companies accordingly break NEDs' fees down into:

- a basic fee;
- additional fees for committee membership (e.g. remuneration or nominations committee);
- further fees for the responsibility of chairing a committee.

In line with the Smith guidance (annexed to the Combined Code), companies should consider paying a premium for membership and chairmanship of the audit committee.

If companies benchmark their NEDs' fees against those paid by other companies, they will typically look at companies where non-executives have comparable time commitments. Survey data on NEDs' fees is differentiated on this basis.

Other considerations

Articles of association

As noted in chapter 4, a company's articles may limit the amount the company can pay in directors' fees. NEDs' fees will count towards this limit, and the articles should therefore be checked when additional non-executives are appointed or when fees are reviewed.

Shares and share options

The Combined Code and the ABI and NAPF guidelines are all strongly against participation by non-executives in **share options**. The rationale for this is that participation in performance-linked remuneration will compromise a non-executive director's independence.

However, some companies will pay all or part of the fees in shares. Both the ABI and the NAPF guidelines **encourage non-executives to use their fees to acquire shares in the company** as this is seen as promoting alignment with shareholders.

7. Design of share incentive plans

This section considers some of the key issues for companies when designing share incentive plans. It describes the different types of plans and performance conditions and looks at their advantages and disadvantages.

Background

Share plans differ from other parts of the remuneration package in several important respects.

Under the Listing Rules, a share plan will **require shareholders' approval** if:

☐ it may involve the issue of new shares or transfer of treasury shares by the company;

☐ it is a "long-term incentive scheme" in which the directors can participate (i.e. it is conditional on service and/or performance over more than one financial year).

These requirements for shareholder approval have been unchanged since the mid 1990s.

Institutional shareholders publish specific and detailed guidelines for share incentive plans. This is not just because of the requirement for shareholder approval. Certain aspects of the plans will materially affect their interests: issues of new shares will involve direct dilution of their holdings.

Share incentives deliver rewards if disclosable performance conditions are met. Accordingly, shareholders focus on whether such conditions are, in their view, sufficiently demanding.

Design issues

(i)   Motivation and retention

To serve their commercial purposes – i.e. to achieve and sustain improvements in performance and increase the commitment of individuals to the business and its goals – plans must be valued by participants.

So both plan design and choice of performance conditions are crucial. A clear "line of sight" between performance conditions and rewards will serve the interests of both companies and their shareholders.

Where companies step back and ask "is our plan working?", the answer can result in a bespoke solution. Two examples are the plans introduced by Kingfisher in 2003 and Cable and Wireless in 2006.

☐   Kingfisher's 2003 plan saw the company move from traditional long-term performance plans based on three years' performance to a hybrid deferred annual bonus plan. This plan delivers rewards based on attainment of annual bonus targets. As a retention mechanism, half of all bonus amounts earned must be deferred into shares for a further three-year period (the other half is paid immediately in cash). There is also a linked long-term incentive award, the amount of which is set by reference to the annual bonus result but which can only vest if further TSR targets are met. (TSR is defined in "performance conditions" below.)

☐   Cable and Wireless introduced a very innovative, if not radical, plan in 2006 that won widespread investor support. The plan reflected a strategic shift from overall group performance to separate business unit performance. Cable and Wireless is now one company with two operationally separate entities – a UK business and an international business. The Long Term Cash Incentive Plan valued each business separately at April 1, 2006 and will reward participants for growth in the value of their own business over the periods to March 31, 2009 and March 31, 2010. If the growth in value equals or exceeds a threshold of eight per cent per annum compound, then a proportion of the value above the threshold will generate a pool from which cash bonuses will be paid. Although this is not a share plan in the strict sense, it replaced existing share plans as the long term incentive for executives within the two businesses.

(ii)   Revised accounting treatment of share incentives

The introduction of the international accounting standard IFRS 2 on January 1, 2005 significantly changed the accounting rules for share-based payments. For quoted companies, a new "expected value" charge must now be taken to the profit and loss account for all forms of share incentives. This rule has applied to AIM companies since January 1, 2006.

The effect has been to alter significantly the traditional distinction between share options with a market value "exercise price", which had no profit and loss impact where new-issue shares were involved, and share plans that delivered "free shares", where there was a profit and loss charge based broadly on the value of the underlying shares at the time an award was granted.

Put simply, share options are no longer without cost. Consequently, many companies have been asking whether alternative plans may have more potential to deliver rewards for comparable profit and loss costs. This is reflected in the types of new share plans that companies have been introducing since 2004 (see table on page 139).

(iii) Dilution pressures

Companies have to abide by the restrictions agreed with shareholders on the number of new shares they can issue under share plans. The long-standing limits contained in the ABI's guidelines mean that:

☐ shares equal to no more than 10 per cent of issued share capital are available to be issued as awards under share plans in any 10-year period;

☐ shares equal to no more than five per cent of issued share capital are available to be issued as awards made under discretionary or "executive" share plans in any 10-year period.

(iv) Views of institutional investors

As stated above, in recent years, institutional investors have paid close attention to the performance conditions that companies apply to share incentives. This has resulted in the following developments:

☐ a range and "sliding scale" of performance targets, with full vesting conditional on the attainment of the highest and only a proportion (for example, 25 per cent) vesting for the lowest;

☐ the removal of re-testing of performance conditions, so that if a condition is not met over an initial period the award lapses;

☐ where companies propose Earnings Per Share (EPS) targets, investors will compare these with consensus brokers' forecasts to determine whether the conditions are sufficiently "stretching". (EPS is defined in "performance conditions" below.)

☐ a focus on the size and composition of groups of comparator companies selected for TSR performance targets.

Main types of share incentive plan

There are three main types of share incentive plan currently offered by UK plcs.

(i) Share options

Share options have traditionally been a popular way to motivate employees. They have several advantages:

☐ they are straightforward and generally easily understood by participants;

☐ they mean the interests of employees and shareholders are aligned – participants will want to see continued rises in the company's share price;

- up to £30,000-worth of H M Revenue and Customs approved options per employee are treated as capital gains rather than income for tax purposes and escape national insurance. (Additionally, companies whose gross assets are less than £30m can benefit from the highly tax-efficient Enterprise Management Incentive plans.)

Nonetheless, many quoted companies have chosen to review their share option plans. This is not just because of the accounting changes outlined above. Other factors are involved:

- concerns that share options may not provide an adequate reward or retention mechanism in a sustained bear market;

- as the value of awards depends on share price rises, the number of shares required to deliver a significant benefit can be large, and this can use up a company's available dilution limits;

- performance conditions for share options have become tougher at the insistence of institutional investors (e. g. by removal of re-testing).

(ii) Performance Share Plans (PSPs)

Under a PSP, an executive is granted free shares – provided the company's performance meets a set target, or targets, over a subsequent period (usually three years). New PSPs have been introduced by a significant number of quoted companies since 2004.

Under the traditional accounting treatment of share awards, a PSP involved a profit and loss expense to the company. However, with the introduction of IFRS 2 (see above), this distinction between PSPs and market value options has been lessened; the relative profit and loss costs of PSPs and share options can now be compared.

The main advantages of PSPs are that:

- in contrast to share options, awards retain their value in a bear market and continue to be a useful reward and retention tool;

- they can allow for a closer connection between individual management performance and reward than share options, where the main driver of value – absolute growth in share price – can be affected by general stock market or sectoral movements;

- as awards are free, it is possible to deliver value equal to that of share option plans for fewer shares. This can help preserve a company's dilution capacity.

The main disadvantages are:

☐ most use "market purchase" shares – that is, existing company shares purchased on the market and held by an employees' trust. There will be a cash cost to the company from acquiring the shares to be held in the trust;

☐ most use the market-driven performance measure TSR; executives often regard this as opaque and feel that it does not reflect their performance as directly as EPS growth. Interestingly, companies are increasingly using alternatives (EPS, PBT, revenue growth, cashflow) to supplement (or sometimes replace) TSR as a performance measure for PSPs. This is allowing them to retain the advantage of PSP structures while using performance measures to which executives feel a stronger affinity.

NEW SHARE PLANS INTRODUCED BY FTSE ALL-SHARE COMPANIES

Year	Share options	PSPs	SMPs
2004	24	69	37
2005	21	76	32
2006	13	70	31

* Source: ABI IVIS Service

Share Matching Plans (SMPs)

SMPs are similar to PSPs in that they can deliver free shares to executives. Like PSPs, they have become more popular with quoted companies over the past few years. The accounting treatment of SMPs is similar to that for PSPs. Also, as with PSPs, performance conditions tend to be based either on TSR or on more stretching EPS conditions than have historically applied to share options plans.

"Standard" SMPs work like this:

☐ an executive agrees to defer receipt of a proportion of their annual bonus – or (more rarely) is compelled to do so;

☐ the deferred bonus is invested in shares on the executive's behalf and held in trust for a period, usually three years;

☐ at the end of the period, the executive receives their invested shares plus a matching award of free shares. Often, the match is "net to gross" (i.e. an employee invests from post-tax income but matching awards are of shares worth the gross equivalent);

☐   the vesting of the matching award is subject to the achievement of performance conditions.

The main advantages of SMPs are that:

☐   they act as retention tools during the deferral period: matching awards are generally forfeited on leaving employment;

☐   by investing a proportion of their bonus in shares, the executive effectively pays to participate in the plan and becomes a stakeholder in the future success of the company;

☐   they tend, given the above, to be encouraged by institutional investors.

The main disadvantages are:

☐   executives can view them as over-complex;

☐   the link to the annual bonus can mean awards are low or even non-existent in difficult years – arguably the times when a company most needs to incentivise and retain executive talent;

☐   as with PSPs, there is a potential cash cost to the company and the risk that executives will be dissatisfied with the performance measure.

Performance conditions

The choice of performance conditions is of critical importance.

There are two main types – **Earnings Per Share (EPS)** growth and **Total Shareholder Return (TSR)**. The principal differences between them are outlined below. In addition, there is an important distinction in the ways they are treated under international accounting standards, and this is explained in the box on page 142.

A key development in recent years has, however, been the use of a wider range of measures for performance conditions. Investors are more willing to accept bespoke measures if an appropriate case can be made. Examples of "non-standard" performance conditions used in new plans in 2006 include profits before tax (PBT), return on capital employed, sales growth and free cash flow targets.

(i)   Earnings Per Share Growth (EPS)

EPS targets are usually expressed as absolute growth targets in excess of growth in the retail prices index over the performance period. They are the common measure for share option schemes, where value is contingent on share price rises.

Key advantages of EPS are that:

☐ it is a measure that executives can relate to: it can be directly influenced by the performance of the management team;

☐ it is widely recognised, used both by companies internally and by external analysts;

☐ the level of targets for vesting awards is set by the company; and the initial hurdle is not a median relative to a peer group that the company cannot control.

Key disadvantages of EPS include:

☐ fair, long-term targets can be difficult to set. Performance targets that are company-specific and take little account of sectoral or market trends may prove too difficult – or too "soft";

☐ executives are not rewarded according to how their company's performance compares with that of its peers;

☐ some institutional shareholders fear that EPS is open to manipulation and view TSR as a better means of aligning executives' interests with their own.

(ii) Total Shareholder Return (TSR)

TSR, commonly used by PSPs and SMPs, measures share price growth and dividends. Almost invariably, a company's TSR is compared with that of other companies and ranked. Investors oppose any payment for below median ranking. At median, a proportion of an award will vest (for example, 25 per cent or 30 per cent; possibly less if the award is worth more than 100 per cent of base salary). An upper quartile or higher ranking is required for full (100 per cent) vesting. There is proportionate vesting for achieving rankings between the median and the upper threshold.

TSR targets are typically supported by a secondary target that is a "financial performance underpin", for example, an EPS growth target. Investors are in favour of secondary targets that are company specific to complement TSR, which is market driven.

Key advantages of TSR include:

☐ it aligns the interests of shareholders and executives by linking rewards to the level of returns that shareholders make on their investments in the company. This is particularly important in a PSP or SMP, where executives can benefit even if the share price remains static or falls;

☐ many investors prefer it;

☐ performance is measured on a relative basis, so setting long-term targets is reasonably straightforward – i.e. full vesting occurs at upper quartile performance, partial vesting occurs at median performance, etc.

Key disadvantages include:

☐ while institutional shareholders insist that awards lapse even if the company's TSR performance is only just below the median of its chosen comparator group, a substantial proportion of an award (for example, 25 per cent) can vest at median performance. A small differentiation in performance can therefore have a huge impact on payments to executives;

☐ finding an appropriate comparator group can be difficult;

☐ as the measure is share-price-dependent it is influenced by market sentiment towards particular sectors, which will not necessarily reflect a company's underlying financial performance. Within a peer group, takeovers or mergers can have a disproportionate impact.

IMPACT OF IFRS 2 ON PERFORMANCE CONDITIONS

Under international accounting standard IFRS 2, TSR is treated as a "market-based" condition and EPS as a "non-market based" condition. This leads to an important difference in the way the share plans are charged to the profit and loss account:

☐ there is an initial discount factor for a TSR performance condition in the formula used to calculate the "expected value" charge. This level of charge is then fixed and accrued over the vesting period. There is no ability to "true-up" (i.e. to adjust accruals) where an award does not actually vest because the performance condition was not met;

☐ there is no initial discount for an EPS performance condition. However, in calculating their annual accruals, companies must estimate the extent to which they believe awards will vest, thereby reducing the level of charge. Accruals can be trued-up so that the final level of charge taken is only for awards that vest.

While this is a very important distinction, opinions vary as to whether it means EPS or TSR is the more attractive option.

For example:

☐ certain companies will prefer to use EPS as they wish to have a charge only for awards that vest;

☐ others will prefer to use TSR – the fixed nature of the charge means that the effect on profit and loss will be less volatile.

interests, insiders and insurance

CHAPTER 7

1.   Introduction

As chapter 2 made clear, directors owe duties to shareholders and others to:

☐   act within their powers;

☐   promote the success of the company;

☐   exercise independent judgment;

☐   exercise reasonable care, skill and diligence;

☐   comply with laws relating to health and safety, competition and tax etc.

These duties are integral to the role of a director and must be fully understood by all members of the board. They are not, though, the full story. There are further duties relating to a director's dealings with the company and transactions in which both the company and a director have an interest.

Essentially, these duties arise from the principle that directors must serve the interests of the company, rather than their own personal interests, and must not abuse their position "inside" the company for personal gain. They may be amplified by the articles of association and, in the case of a listed company, be given additional force by the Listing Rules. Before a transaction can go ahead, therefore, thorough checks will have to be made to ensure it complies with all the relevant rules.

This chapter provides guidance on the types of dealings by directors that are permissible and those that are not. It also looks at ways of protecting directors when any of their duties are breached.

2.   Conflicts of interest

As with the directors' duties examined in chapter 2, the Companies Act 2006 has codified the old law on conflicts of interest, replacing some of the (at times) confusing judge-made law with new rules set down in statute. The new law builds on what has gone before, but, at the same time, can be seen (in places) as a break with the past. What follows describes the regime effective from October 2008.

First, there is a statement of the general duty on a director to avoid a conflict with the interests of the company. A director must avoid a situation in which:

"they have, or *can have* a direct, or *indirect* interest that conflicts with the interests of the company, *or that may possibly conflict* with those interests."

This is broad drafting, catching both actual and potential conflicts and both direct and indirect interests. At first sight, it threatens to paralyse the board. How can directors fulfil this duty without decision-making grinding to a halt?

Fortunately, there is some relief. There is no breach of duty if the situation:

☐ cannot "reasonably be regarded as likely to give rise to a conflict" – if the director's potential interest is so indirect or remote that no reasonable person would see a problem, it can be ignored;

☐ has been authorised by the rest of the board. (Note that the interested director cannot vote or be counted in the quorum for the meeting.)

The articles need to be checked on this latter point. A private company's board will be able to authorise the conflict unless its articles say otherwise. But the rule is different for a plc: the other directors will not have the ability to "nod through" a conflict unless the articles give them specific power to do so.

If neither get-out is available, the conflict must be avoided.

In practice, the duty means that a director cannot, without the company's consent:

☐ compete with the company for a commercial opportunity;

☐ use for their own purpose information belonging to the company;

☐ make a gain from their role.

These restrictions apply even if the company has no wish to pursue the opportunity or is unable to benefit from the information or gain. A director, it should be remembered, is like a trustee; they must remain focused entirely on the interests of the company; no personal interest can be allowed to deflect that focus.

Where the possible conflict arises because the director and the company are going to enter into a contract or some other arrangement together, this rule falls away and is replaced by an obligation to disclose the interest.

3.   Directors contracting with their own company

If the basic principle is that a company and its directors should not have conflicting interests, it must follow that there should be restrictions on them entering into a contract with each other.

Under the old law, a company and a director needed to get shareholder approval before entering into a contract. But most articles would vary that, replacing it with a requirement that the director first declares the interest in the contract to their fellow directors. The new law recognises that fact.

Duty to declare interest in a proposed transaction or arrangement

Unless a company's articles impose a stricter rule such as shareholder approval, the only requirement now is for the director to declare their interest (whether direct or indirect) in the proposed transaction or arrangement before the parties sign up to it.

That declaration is made to the other board members. It can be given orally at a board meeting, or in writing (hard or soft copy) sent to each director. Where there is a continuing interest, perhaps as a shareholder or director of another company, the director can give a general notice saying that they are to be regarded as having an interest in any transaction or arrangement entered into with that other company. If, once made, the declaration becomes inaccurate, it must be updated.

No declaration is needed where:

- the director was not aware of their own interest;

- the director was not aware of the transaction or arrangement with the company (and in both cases that lack of awareness is reasonable);

- the interest cannot reasonably be regarded as giving rise to a conflict;

- the rest of the board are already aware of the director's interest (or they ought to be aware of it);

- the interest arises from the director's service contract – a contract that has either already been considered by the board or a board committee or is due to go before them.

Duty to declare interest in an existing transaction or arrangement

If a director fails to declare an interest when a contract is at the proposal stage, they must do so once the transaction is entered into. The declaration must be made as soon as reasonably practicable. The requirements for the notice are similar, and the same exemptions apply.

But there is an extra penalty for breach of this duty. **Failure to declare an interest in an existing transaction or arrangement is a criminal offence, punishable by a fine.**

4. Duty not to accept benefits from third parties

Taking a bribe from a supplier is clearly wrong. But what about accepting an invitation to Wimbledon or Ascot? The phrasing of a new duty in the Companies Act 2006 gives the corporate hospitality industry pause for thought.

A director must not accept a benefit from a third party that was offered because of the director's position or because of anything the director may do or not do. If a large contract is up for tender, the director who will make the decision should not accept any benefit from one of the potential bidders. There is no need to show that the company has suffered harm: the duty is a matter of principle.

A director is free to accept the benefit if no reasonable person would see it as giving rise to a conflict, but that may not always be an easy call to make. Turning down offers of lavish corporate hospitality may prove to be the safer course.

5. Consequences of breach

What can a company do if a director breaches a duty? There is a variety of possible remedies.

Where a director is exploiting an opportunity or other "property" belonging to the company, an injunction might be obtained to stop the offending acts. And if profits have been made from those acts, a court can order that they be paid over to the company.

A contract entered into in breach of duty will be void unless ratified by the company. Or it may be rescinded if the director failed to declare an interest. If the company will not take action against a director, the shareholders may be allowed to launch a claim in the company's name – see the section below.

Rather than take action against a director, the shareholders can ratify the breach. An ordinary resolution (passed by a simple majority – see chapter 1, section 5) is all that is needed, though the director and their family and other connected persons cannot vote any shares they may hold.

6. Shareholder claims

If the board will not pursue a proper claim against a director, the courts may, as we've seen in chapter 2 (section 8), allow a shareholder to launch a claim **in the name of the company**. The distinction is important: the shareholder is not claiming in their own name for their own loss; rather, they are claiming in the company's name for the company's loss. It follows that any sum recovered goes to the company (and it will be the board's decision whether to pass the benefit on to shareholders by way of dividend).

These principles were established over 150 years or so by judges deciding the cases before them, and the resulting body of law was in places confusing and uncertain. The Companies Act 2006 tidies up the rules under the heading **derivative claims**, the technical term for this type of legal proceeding.

Derivative claims: more power to the shareholder?

Derivative claims by shareholders against directors are not new, but the new set of rules in the Companies Act 2006 has raised their profile. Consequently, there are fears that:

- ☐ activist shareholders (perhaps with experience of the US courts) seeking to persuade a board to sell a business or enter into a merger will use the claims as a tactical device to put pressure on nervous directors;
- ☐ directors will, under the threat of personal liability for some imagined wrong, quickly accept whatever the loudest shareholder calls for.

Given the safeguards built in to the procedure for making a claim, those fears seem unlikely to be realised. To summarise:

- ☐ the shareholder has to have a prima facie case – frivolous or time-wasting claims will go nowhere;
- ☐ the success of the company remains paramount – litigation will only go ahead if it's genuinely in the company's best interests;
- ☐ the shareholder must be acting in good faith in the interests of the company as a whole;
- ☐ the views of other shareholders will be taken into account, and an ordinary resolution in favour of the directors will trump all opposition;
- ☐ a shareholder without a good case will be at risk on costs, its own and the company's.

The courts will not second guess a board decision taken in good faith that appeared reasonable at the time, whatever may have transpired subsequently. Nonetheless, the advent of this new procedure is another good reason for directors to look again at their insurance policies (see section 16).

These new rules (in force from October 2007) apply not just to a director's breach of the duties described in this book but also to a director's negligence and any other failure that may have been committed. There is no need to show that the director has benefited personally, and both present and past directors may be pursued. **Shareholders can use the procedure to pre-empt an action or a future failure, as well as to claim for shortcomings in the past.**

So what exactly is the procedure? A shareholder dissatisfied with a board's lack of action against an errant director must issue a claim in the name of the company and request the court's permission to take the claim forward. A successful shareholder will be allowed to pursue the claim (with the company footing the bill), but the court has a wide discretion to adjourn the case to gather evidence from the company itself. An unsuccessful shareholder risks paying the other parties' costs and an order restraining further action.

Crucially, permission to pursue claims will only be granted if the court decides there is a prima facie case to answer. How will a court decide whether that prima facie case exists? The following are the key criteria:

☐ would a director acting in accordance with the duty to promote the success of the company (see chapter 2) continue the claim?

☐ is it in the best interests of the company to pursue the matter through the courts; or does the shareholder have their own agenda/ulterior motives?

If the decision is that the responsible director would drop the claim, the case must be dismissed.

Other factors to be taken into account include: whether the shareholder is acting in good faith in bringing the claim (or just being vexatious); the views of other shareholders who have no personal interest in the claim.

If the shareholders authorised the act complained of in advance, or they ratified it after the event, that is enough to stop the claim in its tracks.

Because the shareholder is claiming for the company's loss, not its own, it is irrelevant whether it has a million shares or just one, and whether it has owned those shares for decades or just days. Consequently, it's possible for a lobby group that objects to a company's environmental policies, say, to buy one share and launch a derivative claim against the directors for breach of duty. The fact that the harm complained of occurred before it became a shareholder is irrelevant. The directors' defence will depend in part on some of the considerations discussed in the box on page 148.

7. Substantial property transactions

If a transaction between a director and their company is above a certain value, the Companies Act 2006 (s.190, repeating much of the old law) requires that it is approved by shareholders. A director cannot enter into a contract to acquire anything of substance from the company or sell anything of substance to the company unless shareholders have approved the deal in an ordinary resolution or the contract is conditional on getting that approval.

For this requirement to bite, the asset being bought or sold must have a value of more than £100,000 or 10 per cent of the company's net asset value as shown in its last accounts – where 10 per cent is equivalent to at least £5,000. Note that although the requirement for shareholder approval is often referred to as applying to "substantial property transactions" it does not relate exclusively to land and buildings. Any non-cash asset – for example, a trademark – can be included.

The rule can be of particular relevance where a director is leaving a company, and part of the termination package includes the transfer of a company asset, perhaps a niche business in which the director has been working or a property they have been living in. But it does not apply to payments due under a director's service contract or to payments for loss of office.

The need for approval extends to transactions between a subsidiary and a director of its holding company – in which case, the shareholders of the holding company have to back the deal as well. It also applies to transactions between a company and a person who is connected with a director of the company (or its holding company) such as a family member or another company in which the director has at least a 20 per cent interest.

If requirements for approval are not met, the company has the option of setting the contract aside – i.e. making it void. In any event, without shareholder approval, the director is liable to the company for any profit they make on the contract and must indemnify the company for any loss it suffers.

8. Contracts with listed companies

Yet a further set of requirements applies to companies whose shares are traded on the main market of the London Stock Exchange. Chapter 11 of the Listing Rules stipulates that where a transaction is proposed between a listed company or any of its subsidiaries and a "related party", the company must send a circular to its shareholders explaining and valuing the transaction, and convene a formal shareholder meeting to get their approval for the deal.

For these purposes, a related party includes:

- ☐ a director of the company (including a shadow director);

- ☐ a director of another company in the same group;

- ☐ a holder of 10 per cent of the shares in the company or another company in the same group, or someone able to control 10 per cent of the votes attaching to those shares;

- ☐ someone who is no longer such a director or shareholder but was in the previous 12 months;

- ☐ a 50/50 joint venture partner with the company;

- ☐ someone who exercises a significant influence over the company;

- ☐ anyone connected with any of the above, such as immediate family, trustees or a related company.

Exemptions from the requirement for a circular and shareholder vote apply in a number of circumstances. These include those listed below.

- ☐ The transaction has a revenue rather than a capital nature and is "in the ordinary course of business". (Thus, shareholder approval would potentially be needed for a director buying a fixed asset from a listed company for £500,000, but not for the directors to be paid an annual bonus of £500,000 if the bonus scheme could be said to be in the ordinary course of business.)

- ☐ The director or 10 per cent shareholder qualifies as a related party only by virtue of being a director or shareholder of an "insignificant subsidiary" – that is, a subsidiary that has contributed less than 10 per cent of profits and represents less than 10 per cent of assets of the listed group in the past three financial years.

- ☐ The proposed transaction is a "small transaction" – that is, one where various ratios detailed in the Listing Rules (for example, the amount to be paid under the transaction relative to the market capitalisation of the listed company) are no more than 0.25 per cent.

- ☐ The proposed transaction is outside the definition of small because one or more of the ratios detailed in the Listing Rules is above 0.25 per cent but all of them are still below five per cent. In this case, a company will be exempt from the normal requirements, but will have to obtain from an appropriate adviser confirmation that the terms of the proposed transaction are fair and reasonable so far as the shareholders are concerned. (Similar ratios apply to AIM companies. If any of them are five per cent or more, an AIM company must announce the transaction with the related party, disclosing certain specified details about it, and the board must confirm that, having consulted the company's nominated adviser, they consider the transaction to be fair and reasonable.)

9. Loans to directors

As a general rule, it has been unlawful for a company to:

- ☐ lend money to one of its directors, a director of its holding company or a shadow director;

- ☐ guarantee a loan to such directors or provide security for it.

(Unlawful loans or guarantees can be set aside at the behest of the company, and those who benefited from it, or authorised it, are liable to account to the company for any gain they have made and to compensate the company for any loss or damage it has suffered.)

In the case of a public company, a breach of these rules has been a criminal offence, punishable by a fine and/or imprisonment for up to two years.

With the Companies Act 2006, however, the position changed. Under rules in force from October 1, 2007 the total ban goes and loans and similar transactions with directors are permitted if a memorandum setting out the terms and purpose of the loan has been made available to the shareholders and they have given their approval. Where the borrower is a director of the lender's parent company, the parent's shareholders must also give consent.

This is a useful relaxation of the old rule for smaller companies, which have often found themselves tripping over the ban on loans to directors; but a company with a larger shareholder base is less likely to risk members' wrath trying to explain why such loans are necessary.

This restriction on loans is not absolute. A company can:

- ☐ make loans to a director up to an aggregate total of £10,000;

- [ ] ignore the prohibition if it is in the business of lending money and it makes loans to directors on terms that are no more generous than might be offered to an outsider. (A director may be given a cheap mortgage provided the terms are no more generous than those offered to other employees, and the loan is for the director's only or main residence);

- [ ] make loans to a director of a subsidiary, or of a fellow subsidiary, so long as the director is not also a director of the lending company;

- [ ] make loans to directors for the purpose of defending claims made against them by third parties in connection with their position as directors – or even by the company itself. (Shareholders would, though, be likely to question the company's decision to fund the defence to its own claim.) Loans to fund defence costs in regulatory proceedings are also permitted.

If the company in question is a plc, or is in the same group as a plc, the requirements are more stringent. The prohibition will extend to loans to people "connected" with a director (for example, family members, a trustee for a director or their associated company). In addition, the company will be prevented from making "quasi-loans" and entering into credit transactions and related guarantees and security. This may catch expenditure by a company on behalf of a director that is subsequently reimbursed, or use of a company credit card for personal expenditure.

Note that, even where a loan to a director is allowed, it may still need to be disclosed in the company's accounts. In other words, it is not acceptable to keep loans to a director confidential.

10. Disclosure in the accounts of interests in contracts

Companies are required to show in the form of notes to the annual accounts information on transactions between the company or any of its subsidiaries and the directors of the company. This is true whether or not the transaction escapes the three-fold prohibitions and restrictions in companies legislation, the Listing Rules and a company's own articles.

As well as the loans and quasi-loans and indemnities discussed elsewhere in this chapter, details are required of any transactions or arrangements between the company or a subsidiary and a director of the company or its holding company if the director's interest amounted to a "material interest".

What is "material" is a question for the board to decide when putting the accounts together. If the board's decision is reasonable and made in good faith, it cannot be challenged.

The obligation to disclose goes away if a director's transactions and arrangements in a financial year add up to no more than the higher of £1,000 and one per cent of the company's net asset value – subject to an overall limit of £5,000.

This disclosure rule may be a relevant factor in deciding whether or not to go ahead with a transaction.

11. Disclosures in relation to shares

The Companies Act 1985 obliged every UK company to keep a "register of directors' interests", recording the interests that each director (and shadow director) had in the shares of the company or its holding company. Directors had to disclose those interests to the company to allow the register to be kept up to date.

Those rules disappeared in April 2007 and are not repeated in the 2006 Act. Nonetheless, the director of a fully listed company remains obliged to notify their company of any dealing in its shares within four business days, and the company must pass that information to the market by the end of the following business day. The grant and exercise of share options are also disclosable. Similar rules apply to share dealings by directors of AIM companies.

In the case of a listed company, this obligation to disclose share dealings extends beyond directors to other "PDMRs" – that is, persons discharging managerial responsibilities, namely senior executives who make management decisions and have regular access to inside information.

Prospectuses, listing particulars, admission documents and certain circulars produced by fully listed and AIM companies will also require details of directors' interests in the company's shares.

Where the company's shares are traded on the full list, AIM or PLUS markets, a director whose voting rights in the company's share capital reach three per cent or more has a separate obligation to give notice to the company of that interest. (This applies to all shareholders, not just directors.) The company must in turn make an announcement of the notifications it receives about such substantial interests in its shares.

12. Restrictions on dealings in shares

Directors of companies with shares quoted on a stock exchange are obliged not only to disclose details of their dealings, but also to observe restrictions on when they can buy and sell shares in their company. (There are few restrictions on when shares in an unquoted company can be bought or sold, but a director may have entered voluntarily into a "lock-in" agreement not to sell their shares for a certain period, and many unquoted companies will have restrictions in their articles or in a shareholders' agreement that limit the ability to transfer shares freely.)

There are three separate regimes that potentially restrict a director or a senior manager of a fully listed company (or a director of an AIM company) from dealing in the company's shares:

- ☐ that governing insider dealing;
- ☐ that governing market abuse;
- ☐ the Model Code.

These regimes can overlap: more than one of them might apply to a single set of facts. Moreover, their reach is potentially wide. They relate not just to directors but also to senior managers below board level, and indeed, in some circumstances, to any employee who has unpublished price-sensitive information about their company when they deal in its shares. A humble lab technician in a pharmaceuticals company who sees that the final tests on a new wonder drug are not going well might be just as liable as a director who deals before a profits announcement. So the rules on share dealing need to be widely known and understood throughout the organisation.

13. Insider dealing

Insider dealing has been a criminal offence since 1985 and forms part V of the Criminal Justice Act 1993. It is, though, a tricky area. To some, it is just a name for what everyone does and for what makes the City work as a true market. To others, it is an abuse – an inversion of the principle that all potential investors should have the same access to information.

The first legislation to create a level playing field proved ineffective. Since then, efforts have been made to tighten up the law and close the loopholes but there remains a perception that some "wrongdoers" continue to escape conviction.

The attempt to come up with effective legislation in this difficult area means the offence is a complex one to describe; what follows should be taken only as a summary of the main elements. References are made to shares but the legislation also covers other company securities such as warrants, debentures, futures and contracts for differences.

A person will commit the criminal offence of insider dealing if they have inside information and:

- that information is price-sensitive in relation to shares;

- they deal in those shares, or encourage someone else to deal in those shares or pass inside information to another person;

- the dealing takes place on a regulated market or through a professional intermediary such as a broker. (Included in the definition of a regulated market are exchanges elsewhere in the European Union and some other overseas markets.)

"Inside information" is information relating to a particular company that would, if published, be likely to have a significant effect on the price of shares in the company. It will not necessarily be about the company the insider works for: it might be about a supplier or a competitor – for example, news of the winning or loss of a big contract.

The insider will not commit the offence if they pass on general information about the market a company operates in, however confidential it might be. A director of a house building company might be liable if they give their dentist the unpublished information that group sales were significantly ahead of market expectations; but not if they disclose advance knowledge of a rise in mortgage rates.

Transactions that do not take place in the market or through a professional intermediary are safe. This means that the exercise of a share option, a gift of shares or a transfer of shares between family members cannot amount to insider dealing.

There are several other defences available to someone charged with insider dealing:

- they did not expect the dealing to result in a profit by virtue of the price-sensitive information;

- they reasonably believed that the information had been disclosed widely enough to avoid prejudicing other parties to the share transaction;

- the person who bought or sold the shares would have done so without the information – because they needed to sell the shares to raise the cash, or to come within a permitted dealing period etc.

If successfully prosecuted, insider dealing can result in a fine and/or up to seven years' imprisonment. Prosecutions can only be brought with the consent of the Department of Trade and Industry (DTI) or the Director of Public Prosecutions. It should, however, be noted that the Stock Exchange will spot unusual share price movements, make investigations and pass the results to the DTI.

14. Market abuse

The patchy record of the insider dealing regime in stamping out unfair market practices was a factor behind the introduction, on December 1, 2001, of the new civil offence of market abuse. On July 1, 2005, that 2001 market abuse regime was revised to comply with the EU's Market Abuse Directive.

Compared with insider dealing, market abuse requires a lower standard of proof before sanctions can be imposed – the case has to be proved only "on the balance of probabilities", rather than the higher criminal standard of "beyond all reasonable doubt".

Market abuse is also much more loosely defined than insider dealing. So offences are more likely to be dealt with under the market abuse, rather than the insider dealing, regime – at least in all but the most blatant of cases.

Central to the meaning of market abuse is "behaviour" in relation to shares and other financial instruments that are publicly traded, whether in the UK or elsewhere in Europe. If that behaviour corresponds to one of seven types characterised as being either insider dealing or market manipulation, the civil offence may be committed and sanctions can follow.

The regime will catch anyone who tries to "abuse" the securities markets in the ways described, not just those working in the financial markets or who sit on the boards of quoted companies.

This civil offence of market abuse carries no risk of imprisonment but this is no reason to think it is not taken seriously. The Financial Services Authority (FSA) is keen to pursue suspected cases and can levy unlimited civil fines if it believes abuse has occurred.

We describe the market abuse regime in greater detail in chapter 9, along with the FSA's extensive and rigorous powers of investigation. We also give examples there of some of the market abuse cases the FSA has pursued. These give a good indication of what will happen when abuse is suspected.

15. The Model Code

In order to reduce the risk that directors and senior managers of quoted companies might be thought to be taking advantage of inside information, both the Listing Rules and the rules of AIM require that quoted companies restrict the times at which their directors and senior managers can deal in the company's shares. In the case of fully listed companies, the Listing Rules contain a "Model Code" on share dealing by directors and employees that companies are required to adopt in full (though they may impose more onerous restrictions if they want).

The Code says that a director of a listed company must not deal in shares during a "close period", that is the period of 60 days before the announcement of annual and half yearly results. If a company reports quarterly, a one month close period applies before each announcement other than that for the final quarter; the same restriction does not apply before publication of the new interim management statement, though a cautious approach would adopt it in practice.

This is a simple prohibition: it is taken as read that, during those periods when financial results are being prepared, directors are likely to have price-sensitive information.

Outside those periods, directors are still prohibited from dealing if they have undisclosed inside information (see section 2 of chapter 9). This might be news of a possible takeover, a significant acquisition or sale, or a high-level boardroom departure.

Directors who want to deal in their company's shares must first get consent from their chairman or from another director appointed for the purpose. (The chairman should seek permission to deal from the chief executive, and vice versa.) In principle, consent should not be given during a close period or when inside information exists, even if the director concerned has no knowledge of it.

In any event, directors should not deal in their company's shares on considerations of a short-term nature. An investment of less than one year's duration will be considered short-term, and consent to deal should always be refused in such a case.

These rules can be broken only where a director does not in fact have any inside information and can show a pressing financial need to sell shares, such as a need to realise cash to finance an imminent financial commitment. In that case, the subsequent announcement of the sale to the market needs to detail the exceptional circumstances.

Requests for clearance and the chairman's response should always be made in writing, and records should always be kept. Having been given clearance, you should deal as soon as possible and, in any event, within two business days. Miss that time limit, and you have to re-apply.

Directors need to ensure that people connected with them, such as family members, and investment managers making investment decisions on their behalf, are aware of and follow these restrictions. They also apply to those who discharge managerial responsibilities within the company, and to other relevant employees who may be counted as insiders.

The grant and exercise of share options can be caught by the same rules, and advice should be taken in each case.

16. Indemnity and insurance protection

To what extent can a company protect its directors from some of the liabilities outlined in this chapter and in chapter 2, including any legal costs that might be involved? There are two possible options:

- ☐ giving directors an exemption from any liability to the company and an indemnity against liability to third parties;

- ☐ taking out and paying for insurance against any liability incurred by the directors.

The giving of exemptions and indemnities by the company is restricted by the Companies Act; insurance policies need to be carefully read to ensure they cover the desired risks.

Indemnities

For some time, the Companies Act 1985 prohibited all exemptions by a company in favour of its directors and all indemnities except in certain narrow circumstances. The net result was that companies could only indemnify directors who had successfully defended themselves in either civil or criminal proceedings. They could not agree to indemnify them before the event irrespective of the outcome; and they could not indemnify them after the event if they lost. Any term in the company's articles or in a separate contract with a director that provided to the contrary was void and so unenforceable.

On April 6, 2005, however, the position changed. Now an indemnity will be allowed so long as:

- ☐ it does not cover liability to the company in cases where the company sues the director – only liability to third parties can be the subject of an indemnity;

☐ it does not cover liability for fines for criminal conduct or fines imposed by a regulator such as the FSA;

☐ it does not cover other liabilities (such as legal costs) in criminal cases where the director is convicted, or in civil cases brought by the company where the final judgment goes against the director.

So a company can now give an indemnity that will commit it to pay any or all of the following:

☐ directors' legal costs in civil claims brought by a third party, even if the judgment goes against them;

☐ the costs of any damages or other award made against directors if they lose civil claims brought against them by a third party;

☐ directors' legal costs if they are acquitted in criminal proceedings;

☐ directors' costs in fighting civil proceedings brought by the FSA (for example, for a breach of the Listing Rules).

A company's articles will usually permit the giving of these indemnities. But it is a mistake to think the permission in the articles is all that is needed. A director cannot enforce an indemnity through the articles alone. A separate commitment from the company is needed in a service contract or other document.

The general restrictions on a company making loans to its directors (see section 9 above) does not prevent a company from funding a director's on-going defence costs in either civil or criminal proceedings, provided that the terms on which the funding is advanced require the director to repay the money if they are convicted or final judgment is given against them (Companies Act 2006, s.205). This applies even when it is the company itself that is suing the director.

Any indemnities given to directors have to be disclosed each year in the directors' report that accompanies the audited accounts and their terms have to be made available to shareholders at all times. These rules apply also where one company in a group indemnifies the directors of another.

Whether companies should take full advantage of the reduced restrictions on the giving of indemnities is not a straightforward question. Given their increased liabilities and the perception that litigation against them is growing, directors will be keen to have the benefit of every permissible form of protection. But in setting its policy, a board will need to decide whether it believes it is right to give an indemnity in every case – for example, where a director has clearly acted dishonestly or beyond their authority. If money is advanced to a director to meet defence costs in actions brought by the company, it will be necessary to:

☐ explain the decision carefully to shareholders, who may wonder why the company appears to be helping someone it believes did it harm;

☐ consider how the costs are going to be recouped from the director.

Insurance

A company is allowed to take out and pay for insurance to cover liabilities incurred by its directors. Indeed, doing so can be considered part of best practice. The Combined Code on Corporate Governance, whose guidelines are followed by a wide range of organisations (see chapter 3), states that: "**The company should arrange appropriate insurance cover in respect of legal action against its directors**".

The question of insurance needs to be looked at in the context of any indemnities given by the company, as discussed above. If the company decides to insure, it may want to take out cover in respect of those risks it cannot indemnify its directors against – or chooses not to do so. The company may also want to insure itself for liabilities where it has given an indemnity to its directors.

Whatever the company decides to do, it is important for the board as a whole, and for individual directors, to appreciate that there is no standard insurance policy that answers all needs. The exact terms of a policy will be interpreted restrictively, and so all concerned must have a clear understanding of what is covered and what is not. A director is taking a big risk if they simply assume that a directors' and officers' (D&O) insurance policy is in place and will cover them without taking the time to establish exactly what protection it affords.

A new director should at least establish that the insurer is aware of their appointment and that they will be covered by the policy. And both new and existing directors need to satisfy themselves on the terms of the policy. Some of the key points to consider are listed in the box on the following page.

Like a company indemnity, insurance will not provide a complete safeguard for a director against personal liability. It is only part of the answer. Clarification from the company secretary and, if necessary, from insurance brokers and legal advisers, is advisable where there is any doubt.

DIRECTORS' AND OFFICERS' INSURANCE POLICIES: QUESTIONS TO ASK

☐ Does the policy cover both past and present directors so that a director remains covered once they leave the company for actions during the period of appointment? A claim may not arise for some time after the director has stepped down; to be covered, there will need to be a period of "run-off". How long that run-off cover lasts will be a matter for negotiation with the insurers.

☐ Who is covered? A policy will usually protect those who sit on the main board and those who are also directors of subsidiary companies. It will not necessarily extend to those who are nominated to be directors of joint venture companies or companies in which the holding company has only a minority stake.

☐ How does the policy deal with newly acquired businesses? Does cover only start from the date of acquisition, excluding liability for acts committed before then?

☐ What risks are covered? Few cases go all the way to judgment; most are settled out of court. It is important, therefore, to find out whether claims for sums accepted in out-of-court settlements can be made.

☐ What are the exclusions? Invariably, the policy will not cover fraud, deliberate dishonesty and illegal acts; nor will fines and penalties made by the criminal courts and by regulators such as the FSA be included.

☐ What legal costs and expenses are covered? Will they be paid on an interim basis during the course of a case? Are they recoverable if the director loses? Legal costs for an appeal against a criminal conviction will usually be excluded – the insurer will not pay for you to fight your case all the way to the House of Lords.

☐ Will advisers' costs (both legal and accountancy) also be paid for Department of Trade and FSA investigations?

☐ What about claims made outside the UK? Some jurisdictions may be excluded. For example, a director of a company with operations or subsidiaries in North America may not be covered for actions originating there.

☐ What about claims made against directors by their own company? Some policies will exclude liability for a claim made by one party against another insured under the same policy. (The precise wording of the policy will be crucial here; establishing what is included and what is not will require careful checking.)

☐ Will cover extend to all services provided by the director? A D&O policy will only cover directors for liabilities that arise from their role as directors or officers of the company. It will not extend, for example, to professional services that might be performed for a company by a director who is also a lawyer. The cover might not be effective where a director provides their services to the company through their own service company – in these circumstances, it will be necessary to make sure the policy and the insurers are clear in stating that the use of a service company will not lessen the protection given.

☐ If the company pays the premiums, will the insurance be a taxable benefit for directors? Provided things are properly structured, the answer should be "no"; the point needs checking in each case.

☐ What are the monetary limits on claims? There will usually be a limit per claim, and there may also be a limit per year. This means that a claim could effectively be left uninsured if one or two big claims the same year have used up the sum insured. The more people insured under the policy, the greater the risk of this happening.

☐ What about "excesses" or "deductibles"? Different risks may carry different excesses. Where they apply, are they payable by the company or by the director?

insolvency and financial difficulty

CHAPTER 8

1.   Introduction

The main purposes of this chapter are to provide information on the responsibilities and duties of directors of companies in financial distress and to show how directors can minimise the risks of personal liability in the event of insolvency or financial crisis.

It begins by listing the relevant duties of directors. These duties can be thought of as the legal principles or standards a director will be judged by.

Section 3 explains how the duties are best discharged. It is a step-by-step guide to the actions responsible directors take.

Sections 4 and 5 look at breaches of the duties, at the kinds of legal action that can be brought and at the remedies against delinquent directors.

Section 6 explains the various forms of insolvency procedure – the legal options when a company is no longer able to pay its debts.

The chapter is not an exhaustive study of the law but a summary of the main points. Specific, professional advice should be sought in all circumstances.

2.   Directors' duties

The general duties of directors were examined in detail in chapter 2. Below, we highlight those most relevant in insolvency-related cases.

- ☐ **To consider the interests of creditors above those of members.** When a company is clearly solvent, directors must act in the interests of the shareholders in general. When a company is insolvent, or possibly even when it is of doubtful solvency, the position changes.

- ☐ **Not to act for any personal or additional purpose.** All directors should separate their own personal interest (as shareholder, executive, creditor etc.) from the company's interests. Their duty is to act in the interests of the company. This will mean following the principles outlined in section 3 below.

- ☐ **To take steps to avoid loss to creditors.** Under insolvency legislation, a director will be personally liable for wrongful trading if a liquidator can show that **they knew or ought to have concluded there was no reasonable prospect of avoiding liquidation** but continued to do business as "normal". Liability will not arise if the director can show (to the court's satisfaction) that they took every possible step to minimise the potential loss to the company's creditors. They must be seen to have actively tried to do this.

A director should never allow a company to accept credit if in their view there is no reasonable expectation of the creditor being paid at, or shortly after, the time when the debt becomes due. Anyone knowingly party to a transaction in such circumstances could be ordered by the court to make contributions to a company's assets, and be guilty of the criminal offence of fraudulent trading.

☐ **Not to enter into transactions at an undervalue or make preferences.** Insolvency legislation permits an administrator or liquidator of a company to apply to a court to set aside or vary transactions at an undervalue as well as preferences entered into within a specified period before insolvency proceedings began. (Transactions at an undervalue and preferences are defined in section 5 below.) In setting a transaction aside, a court will make an order to restore the position to what it would have been had the transaction not taken place. This may result in personal liability for the directors of the company and disqualification proceedings against any director responsible for the transaction concerned.

3. Actions that minimise the risks of liability

It is important not only that the steps explained below are carried out, but also that they are seen to be carried out: the behaviour of directors may be carefully scrutinised by a future liquidator or administrator. Actions taken in the interests of a company and its creditors should be methodically documented and explained. All meetings must be minuted. Directors must give reasons for their decisions and cite the advice they have taken.

Directors who can show that they acted in good faith on the advice of suitably qualified professionals will be more likely to avoid wrongful trading allegations – even if the liquidator believes the advice they were given was wrong.

Monitoring the financial position of the company

A director should regularly review the company's financial position in order to assess whether the company is solvent and to determine its prospects of avoiding insolvent liquidation. This will generally involve the preparation of regular statements of affairs and cashflow projections and other current financial information – in collaboration with auditors and other advisers as necessary.

Directors should establish a procedure for the finance director to keep the board informed of the performance and prospects of the company. This will generally involve frequent board meetings.

The directors should be satisfied that, taking into account their duties to creditors, shareholders and employees, the company may properly continue to trade. Each director should carefully consider the company's ability to pay before arranging for the receipt of any further goods or services on credit, and the board should regularly review the company's financial position. These reviews should be fully minuted.

Individual directors should raise any concerns over solvency with other members of the board. If their fears are not heeded, they should repeat them and take steps to protect their own position (see the paragraph on resignation in the box on page 172).

When going through a difficult period, directors must regularly ask whether their company fails the **"solvency test"**. A company will be regarded as insolvent when it is unable to pay its debts or the value of its assets is less than the amount of its liabilities, taking into account its contingent and prospective liabilities.

A company is deemed to be unable to pay its debts if:

☐ a creditor owed more than £750 has served a statutory demand at the company's registered office and the debt has not been paid for three weeks thereafter;

☐ execution of a judgment or other court order remains unsatisfied after a visit from a bailiff or sheriff's officer.

If a company is part of a group, it is important for the directors to think of it as a **separate legal entity**, even where the treasury function is shared. The financial position of each company in the group has to be evaluated separately. This may require a review of facility letters, security, guarantees, joint venture documentation, joint obligations and similar documentation in order to determine the nature and extent of the financial position of each subsidiary.

Taking advice

Directors of a company in financial difficulties often face a dilemma. It seems that they are expected to be neither unduly rash nor unduly cowardly.

Causing a company to cease to trade or putting it into administration or liquidation, or calling in an administrative receiver (discussed in section 6) prematurely can be as damaging to the interests of the creditors as allowing a company to carry on trading against all odds.

Directors must act responsibly, resisting, on the one hand, their natural tendency to be over-optimistic or to refuse to accept defeat and, on the other hand, the temptation to succumb to despair without considering the options available. Their analysis of the company's performance and prospects should be based on up-to-date financial information and should almost certainly involve consultation with professional legal and financial advisers.

It may be essential to involve the **company's auditors** in discussions on the financial position of the company. In addition, specific people may need to be appointed to deal with discussions with the company's bankers and other major creditors.

Lawyers will help determine whether a proposed transaction could be vulnerable as a preference or for some other reason, or is otherwise inappropriate (see section 5). A company might need to retain an **insolvency practitioner** to advise on the strategies available.

Existing advisers can be involved in discussions and in the development of strategy – but only if they are qualified to advise in cases of financial difficulty.

Accurate, complete and up-to-date information and access to financial and legal advice from appropriately qualified professionals will significantly strengthen a director's position. They would, for example, be vital in justifying a director's actions if faced with a claim for wrongful trading.

A court will be reluctant to substitute its own commercial judgment for that of a director unless it considers that no reasonable director could have concluded the action taken was in the interests of the company. In cases where directors have taken the advice of properly qualified, competent professionals, judges are unlikely to claim they know better.

In some circumstances, there may be a conflict of interest between subsidiary and parent or between fellow subsidiaries, requiring separate legal and/or financial advice; for example, where it is proposed to use the assets of a doubtfully solvent subsidiary to secure the parent's indebtedness.

Directors may need to seek advice individually on how to minimise the personal risks involved in the management of a company that is approaching insolvency – see section 4.

Formulating a viable strategy

If the company's performance and prospects demand it, a board should formulate a strategy for restoring a company to a healthy financial position and avoiding formal insolvency proceedings. In general terms, the action plan may involve one or a number of the following:

- ☐ alternative trading strategies;
- ☐ disposals;

- [ ] maximising existing asset values;

- [ ] cutting overheads;

- [ ] delaying capital investment;

- [ ] further bank finance (possibly with a grant of security);

- [ ] converting debt to equity, converting short-term debt to long-term debt, or raising new equity;

- [ ] an informal arrangement with major creditors or voluntary arrangement.

The chosen strategy must have the support of the board (the full board if possible). In addition, its viability must be reviewed by appropriate advisers and its implementation constantly monitored.

At the very least, directors should review the strategy at each board meeting and have grounds for concluding that there is a reasonable prospect of avoiding insolvent liquidation. They should reconsider the factors that underlay the development of the strategy and confirm whether in their view they are still valid. A board might have committed the company to cutting overheads, delaying capital investment, relocating premises, selling part of the business or procuring fresh equity. At each meeting, the board will need to review whether the strategy is being implemented as envisaged and whether the underlying assumptions (for example, as to the value of properties) are still reasonable.

The valuations used should be realistic. The accounting principles upon which assets are valued for the purposes of the annual statutory accounts might not be appropriate. The realisable value of any asset will, of course, depend upon all the circumstances in which the asset is being sold. Discussions with a company's auditors may be helpful on this point.

All decisions made and the reasons for them should be recorded in the minutes, as should any advice taken.

Holding regular meetings

Board meetings and other, more informal, meetings should be held at regular scheduled intervals. All directors should endeavour to be present in person or by phone/conference facility. Detailed minutes should be kept of all meetings and circulated in a timely manner. Additional meetings should be called as and when new significant events occur. Briefing papers should be circulated before such meetings to promote informed discussion. Absent directors should be told as soon as possible of critical decisions taken at board meetings.

Involving all directors

Undoubtedly, the involvement of the finance director and any members of the management team responsible for credit control and assessing the current and future financial performance of a company will be key. Depending on the nature of a recovery strategy, input from sales, marketing and production executives may also assume a greater importance.

In most cases, however, it will be the **non-executive directors** who are best placed to assess whether a company is able to continue trading and, in particular, whether it can justify incurring fresh liabilities. Non-executives bring objectivity, experience and financial independence to the board. Where a company's prospects for survival are uncertain, their involvement will ensure that the interests of creditors and shareholders are not overlooked and will facilitate discussions with banks and other lenders.

Keeping major creditors informed

It is important that the distribution of information to creditors' groups is handled in an orderly way. Information to be released to creditors should be discussed with and, in some circumstances, presented by, the company's advisers. Where a strategy to be implemented requires creditors' support (principally that of the lending banks), a careful and clear presentation is required.

If a company's shares are publicly traded, directors will have to consider the problems associated with the release of price-sensitive information (see chapter 9).

Reviewing financial obligations

A board should ensure that the finance director and company secretary are aware of the need continually to review:

- ☐ the maintenance of capital, as imposed by statute;
- ☐ any borrowing restrictions imposed by the company's articles of association;
- ☐ any financial covenants in the company's loan documentation;
- ☐ any regulatory requirements affecting the company.

Appropriate action must be taken if there is any possibility of a breach.

Making announcements

If the company's shares are listed on the London Stock Exchange, the FSA's Disclosure and Transparency Rules will be relevant. These impose certain obligations on the release of information (see chapter 9, particularly the case notes on pages 184 to 187).

When a company's financial situation deteriorates, certain announcements have to be made to avoid the creation of a false market in the company's shares. Announcing that a dividend might not be paid on a listed preference share, or that a company is in discussion with its bankers, will obviously have a marked effect on creditor confidence. Therefore, directors will need to consult their advisers about the timing of announcements.

In addition, directors must be aware that they can be guilty of **a criminal offence** if they:

☐ make any statement, promise or forecast they know to be materially misleading, false or deceptive;

☐ recklessly make (dishonestly or otherwise) any statement, promise or forecast that is materially misleading, false or deceptive;

☐ dishonestly conceal any material facts.

In each of these cases, directors will be guilty if they deliberately induced another person to deal in securities in a company on the basis of false information – or they were careless about what they said and its effect on investor behaviour.

4.   Personal liabilities

Wrongful trading

In cases of insolvent liquidation, a director or shadow director (see question and answer box, pages 172 and 173) can be required to contribute towards the debts or liabilities of a company. This provision does not merely apply to "trading" activity: any act, or failure to act, that either increases or does not minimise losses to creditors can lead to liability.

The level of personal contribution will be determined by the court; it will reflect the extent to which the company's assets have been depleted by the director's conduct.

As stated in section 2 above, a court may make a contribution order if a liquidator can show that before winding-up began the person **knew or ought to have concluded that there was no reasonable prospect of the company avoiding insolvent liquidation**. The only defence open to a director in these circumstances will be that they took every step they could to minimise the potential loss to a company's creditors. The onus will be on the director to prove this defence.

The other main points about wrongful trading litigation are covered in the question and answer box on pages 172 and 173.

Disqualification

The **Company Directors Disqualification Act 1986 (CDDA)** provides that a director can be disqualified for a minimum period of two years for:

- general misconduct in connection with companies;

- conviction for an indictable offence in connection with the promotion, formation, management or liquidation of a company;

- fraud in winding-up proceedings;

- persistent breaches of companies legislation. An example would be persistent default in filing any return, account or other document with the Registrar of Companies;

- unfit conduct as the director of a company that has at any time become insolvent (i.e. gone into liquidation, administration or receivership).

The object of disqualification is twofold: to mark the court's disapproval and to protect the public. The corollary is that a director can attempt to show that their continued ability to act as a director would carry no risks to the public.

Sometimes, people are allowed to continue to act as directors subject to certain safeguards. There could, for example, be conditions that:

- no cheque or financial agreement on behalf of a company is signed or executed by the director alone;

- any loan owed by a company to the director is not repaid unless all creditors of a company are paid first;

- the director shall not grant or accept any security over a company's assets.

"Phoenix" syndrome

Legislation stipulates that the directors of an insolvent company must not, without leave of the court or approval of creditors, be directly or indirectly concerned in the promotion, formation or management of another company with a similar name within five years of the date of liquidation. These provisions relate to a name or trading name used by the liquidated company at any time in the 12 months before the liquidation.

WRONGFUL TRADING CASES: FREQUENTLY ASKED QUESTIONS

What if I resigned from the company. Will I still be liable?

Resigning will not, by itself, remove liability. In some circumstances, directors will be liable for all debts incurred up to their resignation.

Directors who resigned knowing insolvent liquidation was inevitable will, in principle, only be "safe" if they can show they acted on that knowledge – i.e. took steps to protect their interests and those of creditors. They must have tried to persuade the other directors to follow what they believed to be the right course, perhaps using the threat of resignation as a negotiating tool. They must have expressed their views at a board meeting, preferably after producing a reasoned paper for the board, and made sure the minutes accurately recorded their views. In other words, the resignation must be capable of being seen as a response to a refusal to listen – the last resort of a responsible director.

A director who resigns in an attempt to avoid any future liability but continues to be involved with the management of the company as a shadow director may still be liable.

What standards will I be judged by?

In the first instance, a director is judged by the standards of the "reasonable" director. This means they will be deemed to have the general knowledge, skill and experience that can be reasonably expected of a person carrying out the functions of a director. The mere fact that their own knowledge, skill and experience were inadequate for their role cannot be relied on as a defence. On top of that basic standard, a director will also be judged against the general knowledge, skills and experience they in fact possess. Judgments about the extent of these standards will be made case by case, taking into account both objective and subjective criteria.

Directors with professional qualifications (e.g. accountants) may find that their professional body takes disciplinary action or at least seeks explanations of a director's conduct, particularly in relation to the signing off of previous years' accounts and the concept of a "going concern".

How are shadow directors defined?

A brief description of shadow directors and their legal position can be found in section 4 of chapter 1.

WRONGFUL TRADING CASES: FREQUENTLY ASKED QUESTIONS

The key point is that they can be liable for wrongful trading and be ordered to contribute to the assets of an insolvent company. A holding or parent company can be classed as a shadow director in certain circumstances; so can private equity houses and banks.

Liability arises when the shadow director's influence extends to the whole board. For example, a dominant investor can be a shadow director if the whole board, and not just the investor's representative on the board, was acting on its directions.

Are non-executives liable?

As their involvement may be critical when a company runs into difficulties, non-executive directors may find that they are as much at risk under the wrongful trading provisions as executive directors. This will depend on the circumstances of each case, but getting good advice early is key.

What will the court do?

Once liability is established, the court can order a director to "make such contribution (if any) to the company's assets as it thinks proper". It has complete discretion over the amount. In each case, it is likely to assess the difference between the actual net deficiency to creditors and what it would have been on the date when liquidation first appeared inevitable.

The court should also take account of the level of culpability of a particular director and recognise that other factors may have caused the deterioration in the net deficiency.

If it makes a declaration under the wrongful trading provisions, the court may also make an order to **disqualify the director** from being in any way concerned in the management of a company for a minimum period of two years (see page 171).

What can I do to protect myself?

The answer is found in section three. In summary, it is to act responsibly and with integrity. Take an active role in monitoring the company's financial performance and never be afraid to raise concerns about solvency. Make sure what you say, and what you are told in response, are recorded. If fellow directors refuse to accept that the company is wrongfully trading, take no part in incurring further indebtedness.

Insist that any advice you and the board take is noted. It may be vital in disproving allegations by a liquidator and show that you and your fellow directors had reasonable grounds to believe insolvency could be avoided.

If the business is acquired from an insolvency practitioner it can trade under a similar name provided a notice is sent to creditors making clear who from the old company is involved and what they are doing in the phoenix company. This notice must be circulated before a director of the insolvent company has any involvement with its "namesake", but it does not provide a guarantee that the director will escape personal liability for the debts of the phoenix company. In many cases, a director in this situation should be advised to seek leave of the court before becoming directly or indirectly concerned with the "new" company.

Misfeasance

Under the Insolvency Act, office holders and people involved in the promotion, formation or management of a company can be sued for misfeasance – the misapplication or retention of the company's assets or a breach of a fiduciary or other duty.

Misfeasance actions are brought in the name of the company. This distinguishes them from claims made under the provisions for wrongful trading, transactions at an undervalue and preferences – all of which are brought by a liquidator in their own right.

They are often seen as a simpler and, therefore, speedier means of bringing delinquent directors to book and of assessing compensation and damages.

Fraudulent trading

If any company carries on business with the intent to defraud creditors or for any other fraudulent purpose, a liquidator of the company can apply to a court for a contribution order against any person who was knowingly a party to the offence. Since they require fraudulent conduct – i.e. a deliberate intention to act to the detriment of another party – these types of claim are rare. Nonetheless, they remain a risk for directors who allow a company to continue to trade and incur liabilities when they know there is no real prospect that these will be paid.

Pensions

The Pensions Act 2004 includes provisions that could make a director personally liable for a pension scheme deficit (see part III of chapter 5). The so-called "moral hazard" provisions allow the pensions regulator to serve contribution notices on certain third parties in addition to the company itself. These notices can impose liability for all or part of an occupational pension scheme's deficit and can be served on people (e.g. directors) who have attempted or been involved in an attempt to:

☐ prevent the recovery of the whole or any part of a debt that was due, or might become due, from the employer in relation to the pension scheme;

☐ otherwise than in good faith, prevent such a debt becoming due or compromise or reduce it.

The provisions came into effect on April 6, 2005. However, they can, at the discretion of the regulator, apply to any act or failure to act that occurred on or after April 27, 2004.

While the pension fund itself is an unsecured creditor of a company, any deficit is likely to be large: it should never be ignored. Directors must also be aware of the possibility of conflict of interest where they sit on the trustee board and the board of the company.

Personal guarantees

Generally, directors are not personally liable for company debts. If, however, they have given personal guarantees on company loans, personal liability will be incurred. In some cases, bankruptcy orders may even result.

5. Other considerations

Transactions at an undervalue

A transaction will be regarded as being at an undervalue if the company does not receive any consideration for it – or the value of what it receives is significantly less than the value of what it provides. Examples of transactions at an undervalue include:

☐ making a gift;

☐ selling an asset for a price significantly less than its value;

☐ guaranteeing a debt due from another group company.

A court can set aside a transaction at an undervalue and rule that a director has to help "make good" the difference in value if:

☐ the company is in liquidation or administration;

☐ the transaction was made within two years before the start of the liquidation or administration;

☐ the company was unable to pay its debts at the time of the transaction or became unable to pay its debts as a consequence of the transaction;

☐ the liquidator or administrator has made an application to the court for an order.

If the transaction is with a **"connected person"**, there is no need to prove that the company was unable or became unable to pay its debts. Connected persons are broadly defined: they include directors and shadow directors and their "associates" (employers, close relatives, partners, companies controlled by them or their associates) and the associates of a company (other group companies).

A **defence** will be available if a court is satisfied that a company entered into a transaction in good faith and for the purpose of carrying on its business and there were reasonable grounds for believing that the transaction would benefit the company. This defence protects a wide range of bona fide business transactions that might otherwise be vulnerable.

Preferences

A "preference" occurs when a company does anything, or allows anything to be done, that puts one of its creditors, sureties or guarantors in a better position. Examples of preferences include:

- payment of one creditor in full or in part when others remain unpaid;
- granting security in respect of existing debts;
- agreeing to pay a sum for services significantly more than their value;
- making gratuitous payments to employees.

A preference can only be set aside if:

- the company is in liquidation or administration;
- the preference was made within six months before liquidation or administration – or two years in the case of transactions with "connected persons" (see above);
- the company was unable to pay its debts at the time it made the preference or became unable to do so as a result of the preference;
- the liquidator or administrator has made an application to the court for an order.

A transaction will only be deemed to be a preference (and therefore be capable of being set aside) if a company was "influenced by a desire" to put a creditor or guarantor in a better position. It is not enough for a liquidator or administrator to show that a company was aware that the transaction would put a creditor in a better position – a positive wish to achieve this end is needed. Thus, a transaction made for a proper commercial reason is unlikely to fall within this provision.

A liquidator or administrator will generally look very carefully at transactions that benefit directors or their associates, either directly (e.g. paying directors' salaries or repaying directors' loan accounts) or indirectly (e.g. paying off an overdraft guaranteed by a director). Any requests by banks to secure current loans would therefore need to be examined carefully.

If the transaction is with a connected person, a company is presumed to have been influenced by a desire to put the creditor in a better position.

Void floating charges

A floating charge over the company's assets may be invalid if all of the following apply:

- ☐ the company has gone into liquidation or administration;
- ☐ the charge was created within 12 months before the start of the liquidation or administration – or two years if made in favour of a connected person;
- ☐ the company was unable to pay its debts at the time the charge was created or became unable to do so as a consequence of the charge.

If the charge is created in favour of a connected person, there is no need for a liquidator or administrator to prove that a company was or became unable to pay its debts at the time or as a result of the transaction.

A floating charge will not be regarded as invalid if fresh consideration was provided for the security. The following are regarded as fresh consideration: money paid, or goods or services supplied to a company; the discharge of any of a company's debts; interest payable under an agreement for the payment of money, supply of goods or services or discharge of debts.

It should be noted that under the provisions for transactions at an undervalue, preferences and floating charges, a company is deemed unable to pay its debts if it is proved that the value of its assets is less than the amount of its liabilities taking into account its contingent and prospective liabilities.

Unlawful distributions

Assets may be passed to a company's members only if there are distributable profits (i.e. accumulated realised profits less accumulated realised losses) available for this purpose. If there are insufficient distributable reserves, a transaction with or payment to a shareholder could constitute an unlawful distribution of capital.

Directors of insolvent companies may breach their duties to creditors by making gratuitous distributions of assets. Such breaches cannot be waived by the shareholders.

These principles may also apply to distributions to persons connected with shareholders, for example, other group companies.

6.　Insolvency procedures

The following is a brief summary of insolvency procedures.

Administration

Administration will have one of **three purposes**. These, in order of desirability, are:

☐　to rescue the company as a going concern – as opposed to selling its business and leaving a "shell";

☐　to achieve a better result for the creditors as a whole than if the company were wound up;

☐　to sell the business or its assets in order to pay secured and/or preferential creditors (e.g. employees owed wages/holiday pay).

Administrators can only opt for the second purpose if they think that the first is not likely to be achieved or is not in the best interests of the creditors as a whole. They may not seek to achieve the third (fallback) purpose unless they think neither the primary nor the secondary purpose is likely to be achieved and no unnecessary harm will be caused to the interests of creditors as a whole.

The **advantages of an administration order** are that, while it is in force:

☐　a company cannot be wound up;

☐　no legal proceedings can be taken against a company;

☐　a receiver cannot be appointed and no other steps can be taken to enforce any security;

unless, in each case, the administrator consents or the court gives leave.

Once an administrator has been appointed they will take over the management of a company. This will relieve the directors from taking the critical day to day decisions and therefore minimise any risks of liability from that point on.

There are now three **methods of appointing an administrator**. These are explained opposite.

(i) Appointment by the court

A company, its directors or one or more creditors can apply to the court for the appointment of an administrator. The court may appoint an administrator only if it is satisfied that a company is, or is likely to become, unable to pay its debts and that the administration order is reasonably likely to achieve one of the three potential purposes explained above.

(ii) Appointment by the holder of a qualifying floating charge (QFC)

A QFC is a floating charge over the whole or most of a company's property and is created by a document that states that paragraph 14 of Schedule B1 to the Insolvency Act 1986 applies – or, more specifically, that the holder of the floating charge may appoint an administrator or an administrative receiver (if the floating charge was created before September 15, 2003).

(iii) Appointment by the company or its directors

A company or its directors can appoint an administrator without a court order – i.e. make an "out of court" appointment. They will, however, be unable to do so if within the previous 12 months any of the following applied:

☐ the company had been in administration but that administration had come to an end at the behest of the company or its directors;

☐ a voluntary arrangement had ended prematurely;

☐ a moratorium (obtained under schedule A1 of the Insolvency Act 1986) had ended without a voluntary arrangement being approved.

Company Voluntary Arrangements (CVAs)

A CVA is an arrangement whereby the company continues to trade having reached an agreement with its creditors in satisfaction of its pre-existing debts, usually for a percentage of their face value. It can be used in cases where a liquidator or an administrator has already been appointed. The directors propose the arrangement and put it before unsecured creditors for approval. Copies of the agreed arrangement are filed at court.

The procedure to put a CVA in place, and the implementation of a CVA, must be supervised by an accountant qualified to act in insolvency matters – i.e. an insolvency practitioner.

A CVA is not necessarily a "once and for all" solution. A creditor may subsequently apply to a court on the grounds that there is significant irregularity with the CVA or that their interests are being prejudiced.

Until a CVA takes effect, a company will be unable to prevent creditors from enforcing their rights unless additional protection is sought from the court.

Voluntary winding-up

There are two types of voluntary winding-up. Both have the same result: bringing the life of a company to an end.

☐   A **members' voluntary winding-up** depends on a declaration of solvency by directors. The directors swear that they have made a full inquiry into the company's affairs and have concluded that it will be able to pay all its debts, together with interest, within 12 months of the declaration. The company, at a general meeting, then passes a special resolution to wind the company up and appoints an insolvency practitioner as liquidator.

☐   A **creditors' voluntary winding-up** is begun by the shareholders, who pass a resolution saying that the company cannot by reason of its liabilities continue its business and that it is advisable to wind it up. Subsequently, the creditors' wishes regarding the appointment of the liquidator and the conduct of the winding-up generally override the shareholders' wishes.

Compulsory winding-up

A compulsory winding-up can be started without the involvement of a company's shareholders. A petition is filed at court, and at a hearing some weeks later the court decides whether to make a winding-up order. If it does, the company is then in liquidation. The petition is usually filed by creditors.

Receivership

A receiver may be appointed by the holder of a fixed or floating charge granted by a company. Typically, a company will be served with a demand for repayment of monies due, and this will be followed by an appointment just hours later. Alternatively, a company may invite a charge-holder to appoint a receiver.

The receiver's task is to recover sums due to the secured lender or to realise the lender's security.

Historically, an **administrative receiver** has been appointed by the holder of a floating charge covering the whole, or substantially the whole, of the company's property. **Receivers**, by contrast, have been responsible solely for assets subject to a fixed charge.

Administrative receivership, however, is dying out: the provisions of the Enterprise Act 2002 effectively abolished it for charges created after September 15, 2003.

the FSA
in action

CHAPTER 9

1.   Introduction

The Financial Services Authority (FSA) was set up in 2001 as the UK equivalent of the Securities and Exchange Commission (SEC), the mighty US regulator born in the aftermath of the 1929 Wall Street crash. Its duties and powers are the creation of the Financial Services and Markets Act 2000 (FSMA) and numerous pieces of secondary legislation that flow from it.

The authority has four statutory objectives:

- **to maintain public confidence in the financial markets;**
- **to promote public awareness of those markets;**
- **to protect the consumers of financial services;**
- **to reduce financial crime.**

In pursuing its objectives, the FSA may investigate and take action against companies and individuals.

The reach of the FSA is wide, its powers extensive. It is the UK Listing Authority, so all companies listed on the London Stock Exchange are subject to its rules; most companies and senior individuals working in financial services have to be authorised by it and so are regulated by it; it is the investigating and "prosecuting" authority for market abuse, which anyone can commit (see section 3, below).

Successful FSA enforcement action can mean:

- criminal liability – the authority pursues cases through the criminal justice system if it believes it "appropriate" and in the public interest to do so;
- heavy civil fines and/or public censure – the authority can levy unlimited penalties for breaches of its rules and for market abuse (see below) and will publish its findings;
- bad publicity and loss of reputation.

As stated in section 16 of chapter 7, it is impossible to insure against the risk of an FSA fine – though you can take out cover for the costs of defending yourself against FSA action and for compensation to third parties such as customers and investors.

How can people be sure they are toeing the FSA line? The authority sets out the many relevant rules in a handbook, available – along with other useful guidance – on its website.

The information given in this chapter – and the case studies that support it – should provide a guide to some of the circumstances that lead to FSA action against companies and their directors. Expert professional advice will, however, need to be sought in all cases.

2. Breach of disclosure obligations

Disclosure and Transparency Rules

On July 1, 2005, the FSA handbook was restructured to include a new "block", the Listing, Prospectus and Disclosure Rules. On January 20, 2007, the Disclosure Rules were renamed the Disclosure and Transparency Rules (DTR), bringing into UK law provisions from the EU's Transparency Directive and designed to ensure greater transparency as to the ownership and control of corporate entities. They include obligations for companies with a full listing on the London Stock Exchange to disclose to the market information that may affect the price of their shares. Principle 4 of the Listing Principles, designed to ensure adherence to the spirit as well as the letter of the DTR, makes the policy clear: **a listed company must communicate information to holders and potential holders of its listed equity securities in such a way as to avoid the creation or continuation of a false market.**

A core obligation is set out in DTR 2.2.1: a company must notify the market, through a Regulatory Information Service (RIS), as soon as possible, of any **inside information** concerning the company. (The FSA maintains a list of approved RIS providers, which disseminate information from listed and AIM companies for onward transmission to the market.) AIM rule 11 is in similar terms.

Inside information

"Inside information" is information of a precise nature that:

☐   is not generally available;

☐   relates (whether directly or indirectly) to investments traded on a UK regulated market (such as listed shares on the London Stock Exchange);

☐   would be likely to have a significant effect on the price of the shares if it were generally available (FSMA, s.118C).

The price sensitivity of information is crucial. A company must ask: would a hypothetical "reasonable investor", out to maximise their own economic self-interest, be likely to use the information and so have a significant impact on the share price? Information that will usually be considered relevant to a reasonable investor's decisions includes that affecting:

- ☐ the company's assets and liabilities;
- ☐ the performance of the company's business, or expectations as to that performance;
- ☐ the company's financial condition;
- ☐ the course of the company's business;
- ☐ major new developments in the company's business;
- ☐ information that has previously been disclosed to the market.

CASE NOTES: SPORTSWORLD MEDIA GROUP

In September 2001, Sportsworld Media announced that its board was confident that its results for the year ending June 2002 would be in line with market expectations of £14.9m to £18m.

A week later, the board duly agreed budgeted profits before tax for the year of £16.1m. And in the following two months, Sportsworld made further optimistic announcements – results for the year would, it said, be in line with market expectations of around £16m.

On Christmas Eve 2001, the November management accounts were distributed to senior managers, including the chief executive, Geoffrey Brown. For some reason, they did not go to the company's non-executive directors, who received no management accounts from September 2001 to January 2002. Those November management accounts showed that Sportsworld had failed to meet its budgeted profits for every month in the financial year and had in fact made a significant loss for the four months ended November 2001. This meant that to achieve profits of £16.1m for the full year, the company needed to make profits in the second half that were not in the budget agreed by the board.

But Sportsworld and Brown expected to see additional profits from acquisitions in the second half and from adjustments regarding costs in the management accounts. So they concluded that budgeted profits for the full year could still meet market expectations, albeit not in the way they had originally intended.

On January 9, 2002, the company's financial performance was discussed at a managers' meeting at which Brown was present. On January 21, 2002, Brown and the finance director discussed the December 2001 management accounts. Both agreed that their expectations of profit before tax for the year ended June 2002 had now changed but that further work was needed to understand the position properly.

On Friday, January 25, 2002, a board meeting was held to discuss the half-year performance, and the board decided to announce that the company's expectation of its

In addition, a company must **take all reasonable care** to ensure that any information it releases to the market is not misleading, false or deceptive, and that it does not omit anything that is **"likely to affect the import"** of the information (DTR 1.3.4).

Although the rules on the disclosure of inside information have changed, cases decided under the old regime will continue to give valuable guidance as to how these obligations will be enforced.

The FSA – as our case studies in this section show – has been rigorous in its pursuit of errant companies and has used its powers against directors who were "knowingly concerned" in a breach (FSMA, s.91(2)).

---

profit before tax for the year was in the £9m to £10m range. On the following Monday, a trading statement was issued to that effect, and the company's share price fell by 61 per cent.

Matters then went from bad to worse and, on February 13, a further corrective announcement was issued: Sportsworld's results for the year would be substantially below the £9m to £10m range. The company's share price fell a further 87 per cent. In the space of just six weeks – from the end of 2001 to the middle of February 2002 – Sportsworld's market capitalisation had gone from £163.5m to £2.4m. The company's shares were suspended in April, and an administrative receiver appointed.

The FSA concluded that Sportsworld's delay in making an announcement from December 24, 2001 (the date the November management accounts were available) to January 28, 2002 was a breach of the obligation to disclose, as soon as possible, information on the performance of the company's business or on expectations of that performance. It took the view that the market would have reacted materially and adversely had it known that, to deliver the expected full-year profit, Sportsworld was relying on a much more optimistic second-half performance than had previously been budgeted for. It mattered little, in the eyes of the FSA, that the company's subjective expectations of headline profit had initially stayed the same; expectations about how the profit would be phased between the first and second halves of the year had changed, and that would have had a significant effect on the share price if the market had known.

Sportsworld was publicly censured for the breach, and the FSA indicated that if the company had had the resources (by now it was in receivership) it would have been penalised by a substantial fine. The FSA concluded that Brown was "knowingly concerned" in the breach and fined him £45,000. He should, in the FSA's view, have brought the change in the expectation of the company's results for the year to the attention of the full board and otherwise ensured that the company complied with its disclosure obligations.

CASE NOTES: UNIVERSAL SALVAGE

Universal Salvage had a rolling contract with Direct Line Insurance for vehicle salvage that could be terminated on three months' notice. The contract was responsible for approximately 40 per cent of the vehicles handled by the company and for a significant proportion of its turnover.

Direct Line put the contract up for tender and, at a meeting on March 18, 2002, informed Martin Hynes, chief executive of Universal Salvage, that he had lost the business. The Universal Salvage board was told of this on March 20, 2002, and written confirmation of termination was received by the company on March 25, 2002. The termination was to take effect on June 30, 2002. Universal Salvage thought this was a negotiating ploy and wrote to Direct Line raising a number of arguments as to why the contract should continue. Direct Line undertook to investigate the issues raised. Nevertheless, on April 16, 2002, Universal Salvage again received a letter that confirmed the loss.

In the meantime, Universal Salvage had been analysing the financial impact of the termination, all for a presentation to the board on Thursday, April 18, 2002. At that board meeting, it was decided that Hynes should seek advice from the company's financial adviser, WestLB, about the loss of the contract and the poor trading performance the company was experiencing in the final quarter.

The board meeting ended at 1.00pm. Hynes telephoned WestLB at 4.30pm and again at 5.00pm but his usual contact was unavailable. Hynes got hold of him the next morning, Friday, and it was agreed that they would meet on Monday, April 22, 2002. At that meeting, WestLB advised that an announcement should be made to the market about the lost contract and the poor trading figures. The announcement duly followed at 3.45pm on Tuesday, April 23, 2002; the company's share price fell by 55 per cent.

The delay of only five working days in announcing the termination of the contract – from April 16 to April 23, 2002 – was determined by the FSA to be a breach of the obligation to disclose, as soon as possible, a major new development in the company's business. As from April 16, the company needed to win significant amounts of new business to sustain previous levels of turnover and profit, and this, held the FSA, was a material fact, likely to lead to a substantial movement in the company's share price. The authority pointed to the 55 per cent drop in the share price to support its argument.

In addition, the FSA decided that Hynes was "knowingly concerned" in the breach as he was the director best placed to take appropriate steps to ensure that the company notified the market without delay and he had failed to do so.

The company was fined £90,000; Hynes, £10,000.

Personal liability for directors

The definition of "knowingly concerned" is not, on the evidence of existing FSA case material, clear cut. The Sportsworld and Universal Salvage cases suggest that the "guilty"

CASE NOTES: PACE MICRO TECHNOLOGY

On January 8, 2002, Pace announced its interim results but failed to reveal that its trade credit insurance for future deliveries to one of its largest customers had been withdrawn. The FSA judged this to be a breach of the obligation to ensure that information released to the market is not misleading and does not omit anything "likely to affect the import" of information already released.

The regulator held that because two annual reports had previously stated that a credit insurance programme existed for large customers, the loss of cover was material and did affect "the import" of the interim results announcement. It criticised Pace for not seeking sufficient advice on the matter. (The company had talked to its financial adviser but not its brokers.)

The FSA also found Pace to be in breach of the obligation to announce a change to the company's expectations for its revenue performance without delay.

The interim results showed that revenue for the year to June 1, 2002 would be broadly similar to the 2001 figure of £524m. On February 4, 2002, Pace revised its forecast to £455m but failed to inform the market of the change. The company argued that its earnings expectations had not changed (because the lost sales would have produced little or no profit) – and it is earnings, rather than revenue, that would usually be price-sensitive. It was not until March 5 that a trading statement was made – by which time things had deteriorated further and expectations had fallen to £350m. The news led to a share price fall of 67 per cent and wiped £462m from the company's market capitalisation.

The case underlines the need to include all material information when making announcements. The loss of the insurance cover was not deemed to be price-sensitive – just material to the matter being announced.

The FSA accepted that Pace had not acted recklessly or deliberately but had simply come to the wrong conclusion about what was material. The company was nonetheless fined a hefty £450,000 for breaching the two rules.

director does not need to have any intention to mislead the market: knowledge of the facts and some involvement in the breach were enough to result in fines for each chief executive. In the later case of Pace, however, the directors escaped penalties and censure – the FSA seems now to have accepted the idea that to "be knowingly concerned" a director must have some awareness that the company is breaking the rules.

The safest course will always be to make sure you know the rules and assume that **absence of bad faith will not be enough to get you off the hook**. In this context, Listing Principles 1 and 2 are very relevant:

☐   a listed company must take reasonable steps to enable its directors to understand their responsibilities and obligations as directors;

☐   a listed company must take reasonable steps to establish and maintain adequate procedures, systems and controls to enable it to comply with its obligations.

If the FSA cannot pin a breach of a specific listing rule on to a company or its directors, it now has the ability to pursue them for a breach of these listing principles. It could be all too easy, after the event, for the regulator to allege that directors did not understand their responsibilities and obligations, and that adequate systems were not in place for compliance.

Is it just the chief executive who is at risk of a fine? The short answer is "no". All directors of a listed company should accept full responsibility, collectively and individually, for the company's compliance with the rules. Although the FSA decided, in both the Sportsworld and Universal Salvage cases, that the CEOs had a particular responsibility, all directors, executive and non-executive, are under a duty to ensure the company complies with its obligations and to bring any price-sensitive information to the attention of the full board as soon as possible. And, as the Universal Salvage and Pace cases have shown, the FSA will be critical if the board does not seek prompt advice from the company's brokers.

The rest of the board should not simply point to the CEO and expect him or her to take the rap in every case.

3.   Market abuse

Background; the old and new regimes

As chapter 7 explained, the market abuse regime was introduced at the end of 2001 as a means of bringing more people who trade on inside information to justice. It sits alongside the criminal regime of insider dealing but operates with the lower standard of proof required for civil proceedings and potentially covers more transactions. Because it is not a criminal offence, you cannot be imprisoned for market abuse, but you can face unlimited fines and/or public censure.

The FSA has been keen to pursue the more blatant cases of abuse of the financial markets and has brought a number of successful actions against companies and individuals (see the case notes box on page 190 and 191). However, there is at least a perception that the general European record of enforcement of market abuse provisions remains poor by American standards. The chairman of the US Securities and Exchange Commission was able to declare 2006 a "banner year for enforcement" as he boasted that "the SEC went 10 – 0 in trial court wins this year". The FSA can only dream of such a record; in 2006, while the SEC brought 574 enforcement actions, it managed only 109.

The European Commission has moved to improve compliance across Europe with the 2003 **Market Abuse Directive.** This has led to the introduction of a new market abuse regime in the UK, which took effect on July 1, 2005. Many of the features of the new regime correspond broadly to what went before, but it should not be assumed that what was allowed under the previous regime is still allowed now.

The new regime applies to more financial instruments and is wider in territorial reach (see "scope", below). It encompasses both insider dealing and market manipulation and classes seven types of behaviour as market abuse. It should be noted, however, that both insider dealing and market manipulation remain criminal offences.

Anyone may be liable for market abuse, not just those companies and individuals regulated by the FSA. Liability can arise even when the abuse was unintentional or committed indirectly – i.e. through the act of encouraging "abusive" behaviour in another.

This section gives an outline of the market abuse regime. You should consult a financial regulatory lawyer if you are in any doubt about whether a behaviour is caught by the rules.

Scope of the market abuse regime

The market abuse regime covers:

☐ financial instruments (such as shares, warrants, futures, contracts for differences, options and debt instruments) traded on every regulated market in Europe (or for which an application for admission to trading has been made). In the UK, the relevant markets include the London Stock Exchange (both the full list and AIM), PLUS (the old OFEX) and commodity derivative markets;

☐ all transactions relating to those instruments even if they are carried out off-market.

In certain circumstances, behaviour in respect of other, related, instruments or underlying commodities is also caught, even if those instruments are not themselves traded on a regulated market. Behaviour involving securities traded on a foreign unregulated market may be caught if an option linked to them is traded in London.

The seven behaviours

There are seven types of behaviour defined as forms of market abuse.

Insider dealing – dealing or an attempt to deal, by an insider, in an investment on the basis of inside information in relation to the investment.

Improper disclosure of inside information – disclosure by an insider of inside information to another person otherwise than in the course of their employment, profession or duties.

Misuse of information – behaviour that is both:

(a)   based on information not generally available to those using the market but likely to be seen by "regular users" as relevant when deciding the terms on which transactions in investments should be made; and

---

CASE NOTES: EXAMPLES OF MARKET ABUSE

The following are real-life examples of FSA actions for market abuse, showing the risks that companies and individuals can face. They cannot be taken as definitive statements of the law in the same way as a case decided by a court. But they do show the view taken by the FSA of certain conduct and illustrate the penalties that can be imposed.

A simple example of **misuse of information** market abuse is seen in the case of **Jonathan Malins**, the finance director of AIM company **Cambrian Mining**. Having chaired a meeting to approve a share placing at a premium to the current market price, Malins bought shares for his own account that afternoon, less than an hour before the share placing was publicly announced. He pulled the same trick a week later, buying shares immediately ahead of the announcement of better than expected results. These flagrant examples of abuse, which also breached the company's internal rules, netted Malins immediate profits of £6,000 and £400. He was fined £25,000 in December 2005.

A further blatant example is provided by **James Parker**. He was the financial controller at **Pace Micro Technology,** and the facts of the case revolve around the problems described on page 187. With the benefit of inside information and in clear breach of the company's share dealing rules, Parker not only sold shares ahead of the announcement, which led to a dramatic fall in the company's share price, but also carried out an active programme of spread bets on the share price, making an aggregate profit of £121,742. His claim that this was part of an existing strategy uninfluenced by his inside information was not believed, and in August 2006 he was fined £250,000.

(b)   likely to be seen by regular users as below reasonable or acceptable standards.

Manipulating transactions – participating in transactions or orders to trade that give, or are likely to give, a false or misleading impression as to the supply, demand, price or value of a qualifying investment or related investment, or that secure the price of such an investment at an abnormal or artificial level.

Manipulating devices – participating in transactions or orders to trade that employ fictitious devices or any other form of deception or contrivance.

Disseminating information likely to give a false or misleading impression – the act of spreading, or causing the spread of, information about a qualifying or related investment by a person who knew or could reasonably be expected to have known that the information was false or misleading.

The £17.m fine levied against **Shell** in August 2004 for market abuse and breach of the Listing Rules set a new FSA record. In early 2004, Shell announced that it was writing down 25 per cent of its hydrocarbon reserves, causing a £2.9bn drop in its market capitalisation. The FSA found that the company had not only made **false or misleading announcements** in relation to its reserves since 1998 but also failed to act when evidence of irregularities first came to light. In a 17-page document based on internal memoranda, the regulator showed how executives were aware of the problems at least four years previously. Given the FSA's stated view that timely and accurate disclosure to shareholders and markets is fundamental to the maintenance of the integrity of the UK's financial markets, the breach could hardly have been worse. Nonetheless, the FSA fine appeared puny compared with the $120m (£66m) settlement agreed with the SEC. Having ruled against Shell, the FSA continued its enquiries into the conduct of a number of individuals in the senior management at the company, most notably the former chairman, Sir Philip Watts. But in November 2005 it announced that no further action would be taken. The company may have been at fault, but no one individual was found to have committed market abuse.

Distorting the market led to a fine of £500,000 for **Evolution Beeson Gregory (EBG)**, the financial services group, and of £75,000 for its head of market making. EBG also paid £150,000 in compensation to investors. In autumn 2003, the company had short sold more than twice the entire issued share capital of an AIM listed company with, in the FSA's view, no reasonable plan for ensuring its ability to deliver the shares it had sold. An expected issue of new shares did not materialise; 250 investors failed to get the shares they thought they had bought. EBG's trading led to a serious distortion of the market, resulting in the suspension of the shares on AIM.

Market distortion – behaviour that is likely to be seen by a regular user of the market as a failure to observe the standard that could be reasonably expected in the circumstances and that either:

(a)　gives, or is likely to give, a regular user of the market a false or misleading impression as to the supply, demand, price or value of a qualifying or related investment; or

(b)　could be regarded by a regular user as distorting, or being likely to distort, the market in that investment.

The **FSA's Code of Market Conduct**, which can be accessed via the FSA website, sets out further guidance on what is and what is not market abuse.

Safe harbours

There are some "safe harbours" from market abuse. Some actions will not be caught if they comply with other rules – for example, certain provisions of the Takeover Code and the Listing Rules. (Note that there were changes regarding safe harbours with the introduction of the new regime on July 1, 2005.)

Critical factors

When deciding whether or not to take enforcement action on market abuse, the FSA says it will look at a number of factors. These include:

- ☐ the nature and seriousness of the suspected behaviour;
- ☐ the conduct of the person concerned after the behaviour was identified;
- ☐ the degree of sophistication of the users of the market in question, the size and liquidity of the market, and the susceptibility of the market to abuse;
- ☐ whether sufficient action has been taken by other regulatory authorities;
- ☐ action taken by the FSA in previous similar cases;
- ☐ the impact, given the nature of the behaviour, that any financial penalty or public statement may have on the financial markets or on the interests of consumers;
- ☐ the likelihood that the same type of behaviour (whether on the part of the person concerned or others) will happen again if no action is taken;
- ☐ the disciplinary record and general compliance history of the person who has committed the market abuse.

The FSA can impose unlimited fines on companies and individuals found to have committed market abuse. Other sanctions include: a public statement that a person has engaged in market abuse; a court injunction to prevent any repeat; a requirement to give up any profits made or to pay compensation to the victims of any abuse. (The victims have no right of direct action against the abuser under the market abuse legislation.)

In issuing fines, the FSA says it has three main objectives:

- ☐ to send a strong message to directors and senior management of the firm that the behaviour in question is unacceptable;

- ☐ to attract publicity and so threaten the reputation of a company in breach and its "brand value";

- ☐ to provide a general deterrent to the market as a whole.

4. Market manipulation

The civil regime of market abuse described above runs in parallel not only with the criminal offence of insider dealing but also with that of market manipulation (FSMA, s.397(3)).

A person will be guilty of market manipulation if they commit any act or engage in any conduct that creates a false or misleading impression as to the market in any investments, or their price or value, and they do it with the intention of:

- ☐ creating such a false and misleading impression; and

- ☐ inducing another person to deal (or not deal) in those investments.

The "classic case" is that of the share ramping operation, whereby a party drives up a company's share price by buying heavily and so creating a false impression of the demand for the shares – perhaps to influence a takeover where the shares are being used to settle part of the offer price.

Market manipulation can mean an unlimited fine, a prison sentence of up to seven years, or both.

It should be emphasised, though, that there has to be a clear intention on the part of the accused to mislead and for others to rely on the misleading impression. It is a defence to show that you reasonably believed that you would not create a false impression; evidence of full public disclosure of what was being done and by whom will greatly assist your case.

Other defences apply where the action was taken in accordance with rules to control the issue of information (such as the Listing Rules) or in connection with a buyback of shares.

5. Misleading statements

A further criminal offence seeks to catch those who make misleading statements in the financial services sector (FSMA, s.397(2)).

A person can be liable if they:

☐ make a statement, promise or forecast that they know to be materially misleading, false or deceptive;

☐ recklessly make such a materially misleading, false or deceptive statement, promise or forecast – whether they are dishonest or not;

☐ dishonestly conceal any material facts in a statement, promise or forecast.

In each of these cases, the person will be guilty if either of the following applies:

☐ they made the statement for the **purpose** of inducing another to enter into an investment agreement or to exercise (or refrain from exercising) any share rights;

☐ they were **reckless** as to whether the statement would have that effect.

The reference here to entering into an investment agreement is a poor shorthand for the whole panoply of controlled activities regulated by FSMA and the secondary legislation derived from it. If there is any doubt about whether a sphere of activity is caught by the misleading statements provision, professional advice should be taken.

Some of the most obvious cases occur when a company is floating on the stock market. Directors will commit the offence if a statement or a forecast in a prospectus that they know to be false induces investors to take up the shares. Or if they are reckless as to whether the statement or forecast is false – that is, they have taken no care in establishing the truth and have simply shut their eyes to the misleading nature of what is said. Boards and their advisers must take extreme care in producing these kinds of documents, verifying each and every statement that could influence the behaviour of investors. The same applies to documents sent to shareholders on a company takeover, whether by the bidder or the target.

Like market manipulation, the offence is punishable by up to seven years in prison and/or an unlimited fine. But directors who make misleading statements face more than criminal liability. They may also be liable for compensation to investors who lost money.

Both imprisonment and a compensation order were the consequences for two directors of AIM company **AIT** in the first case brought by the FSA under these provisions. **Carl Rigby** and **Gareth Bailey** issued an announcement stating that the company's turnover and profit were in line with expectations. Those expectations depended on revenue from three specific contracts. The problem was that the contracts did not exist. In August 2005, Rigby and Bailey were convicted at Southwark Crown Court of recklessly making a statement that was misleading, false or deceptive and were sentenced to three and a half and two years respectively (reduced to 18 and nine months on appeal). The Court of Appeal upheld a compensation order against Rigby of £208,796 and a costs order of £250,000; Bailey had to pay the more modest sum of £35,114.

6. FSA enforcement procedures

Powers

When investigating cases like the ones detailed above the FSA has a number of statutory powers to assist it.

It can obtain information that is relevant to its inquiry; it can, in certain cases, call on the police to arrest suspects; and it can, in certain cases, detain people for questioning. **Those who are seen to impede or obstruct its investigations can face stiff penalties.** In October 2003, FSA suspect Christopher Westcott was given a 28-day suspended prison sentence by the High Court for failing to co-operate with the authority's inquiry. The FSA had been investigating Westcott, suspected of selling funeral plans without proper authorisation and using a number of aliases to do so, since April 2002. His sentence was suspended only on the condition that he subsequently complied with the FSA inquiry.

The FSA says that it will make it clear in each case whether it is using its statutory powers or not. Where it is not, there is no obligation to produce documents or to attend an interview or to give answers when questioned.

Use of the statutory powers is, however, standard practice. In most cases, parties will be compelled to produce documents and answer questions in interview – even if they are willing to co-operate voluntarily. Consistent use of its statutory powers is, the FSA believes, fairer and more transparent and efficient for all concerned. So finding oneself on the wrong end of the FSA's use of its powers of compulsion does not mean that you are suspected of anything or viewed as being hostile; even innocent witnesses are likely to be subject to this standard practice.

But the FSA is equally clear that **ready co-operation in attending an interview and answering questions may well result in a more lenient penalty should misconduct be found.** Where the statutory powers are used, a failure to attend an interview, as Westcott found, will be a contempt of court punishable by a fine, imprisonment or both, as will a failure to answer questions or to produce documents. There is, in effect, no right to silence. And there is no equivalent to the US citizen's right "to plead the fifth" – that is, protect themselves against self-incrimination.

The FSA's powers are undoubtedly extensive, but it says it does not want to waste them on trivial matters. Its stated intention is to concentrate on the more important breaches rather than try to pick up every minor transgression (see "review", below).

Settlement

A party under investigation can, at any point, open settlement discussions with the FSA and so spare themselves the time, expense and bad publicity of further investigation. The FSA claims it gives credit in deciding penalties for early co-operation and acceptance of fault. In the Shell case (see case notes, page 191), the fine of £17m would have been "significantly higher", the FSA said, had it not been for the company's high degree of co-operation. (Interestingly, Shell did not admit it was at fault.)

Decisions and appeal

If, having made investigations, the FSA decides to pursue a matter, it will take it in the first instance to its Regulatory Decisions Committee (RDC). Staffed by current and recently retired City practitioners as well as by lay members, the RDC oversees the enforcement process; it examines cases and takes representations from parties under investigation. If the firm or individual concerned accepts the committee's decision, it takes effect. If there is no acceptance, and the FSA issues a decision notice, the accused can refer the matter to the Financial Services and Markets Tribunal, an independent body run, like the mainstream courts, by the Department of Constitutional Affairs. Tribunal hearings are conducted from scratch. They usually, however, take place in public – a fact that may argue in favour of settling the case with the FSA.

Review

Following criticisms levelled at the FSA by the Financial Services and Markets Tribunal in the mortgage mis-selling case brought against Legal and General, the authority launched a review of enforcement processes in early 2005. That has led to administrative reforms distancing the RDC from the rest of the regulator's enforcement function. The view at the FSA is that these changes have led to greater transparency and to an increased perception of the fairness of its processes. It remains to be seen how optimistic a view that is.

There has also been a big reduction in the number of cases brought by the FSA – from 600 in 2000 to 109 in 2006. The regulator says it takes a risk-based approach and will now only pursue those cases that are in line with its overall priorities and where it is important to send out a message to the market or where breaches are particularly serious.

7. Lessons to be learned

In reaching the decisions described in the case notes sections of this chapter, the FSA drew the following conclusions:

☐ in respect of **new developments** in its sphere of activity, a listed company must first consider objectively the importance of those developments to the business and then, with its advisers (including its corporate brokers), objectively assess whether they may lead to a substantial movement in the company's share price;

☐ in respect of a **change in the performance** of the business, a listed company must first consider objectively whether there has been such a change and then, with its advisers, objectively assess the likely price sensitivity of the change;

☐ when looking at any **change in its expectations of its performance**, a listed company must first assess whether there has been a change in its subjective expectations (given the relevant facts) and then, with its advisers, objectively assess the likely price sensitivity of any change.

In addition, to minimise their exposure to, and the risk of, personal liability, directors need to:

☐ make sure the company has a **formal documented process** to ensure compliance with its obligations under the Disclosure and Transparency Rules and the Listing Rules;

- [ ] regularly review compliance with those rules and rigorously monitor changes to the company's financial condition, performance and its expectations of its performance;

- [ ] ensure the company and the board are aware of the **consensus of market expectations regarding the company's results** and that they regularly ask whether the company's own expectations are in line with that consensus;

- [ ] keep under review announcements already made and documents already published (such as audited accounts and previous trading statements) and consider whether any later developments may be **material** in the context of that information;

- [ ] ensure that executive directors elevate issues to the full board without delay;

- [ ] make sure that **all members of the board**, executive and non-executive, receive copies of the monthly management accounts and details of any major developments in the company's sphere of activity;

- [ ] seek **prompt advice** from the company's corporate brokers, financial and other advisers as to whether any information or matter is price sensitive.

Companies Act 2006

Implementation Timetable

Change	Page	Implementation date
AGM – not needed for private company	17	Oct 1, 2007
Auditors – limitation of liability	15	Apr 6, 2008
Beneficial owners – exercise of shareholder rights	12	Oct 1, 2007
Business Review – new content	68	Oct 1, 2007
Directors		
☐ one must be natural person	29	Oct 1, 2008
☐ age limit of 70 abolished	30	Apr 6, 2007
☐ minimum age of 16	30	Oct 1, 2008
☐ new code of duties (other than conflicts of interest)	30	Oct 1, 2007
☐ conflicts of interest	144	Oct 1, 2008
☐ shareholders can ratify breach	38	Oct 1, 2007
☐ loans	152	Oct 1, 2007
☐ service contracts, need for shareholder approval	76	Oct 1, 2007
☐ liability for false Directors' Report	39	Jan 20, 2007
☐ liability for false periodic financial information	40	Nov 8, 2006
☐ liability for true and fair view	40	Apr 6, 2008
☐ notification of share dealings – repealed	154	Apr 6, 2007
e-communications with shareholders	19	Jan 20, 2007
Financial assistance – lifting of ban for private companies	4	Oct 1, 2008
Memorandum		
☐ no objects clause	8	Oct 1, 2008
☐ existing objects clause transferred to articles	9	Oct 1, 2008
☐ objects unrestricted	9	Oct 1, 2008
Minutes – retention for 10 years	17	Oct 1, 2007
Notice of meeting – time periods	19	Oct 1, 2007
Secretary – not needed for private company	13	Apr 6, 2008
Share capital		
☐ authorised abolished	22	Oct 1, 2008
☐ allotment authority not needed for private company with one class of share	24	Oct 1, 2008
☐ public company, sterling or euros	3	Apr 6, 2008
Shareholder derivative claims	148	Oct 1, 2007
Takeover Code – put on statutory basis	4	Apr 6, 2007
Written resolutions – reduced majorities needed	21	Oct 1, 2007

index